The Wrestling Insomniac
Volume 2

Michael J. Labbe

Introduction

Thank you very much for taking the time to read my second book The Wrestling Insomniac Volume 2. This volume features more posts from the blog with a theme consisting of championship statistics and detailing wrestler's short runs or final matches. I'd like to thank my buddy Brandon Myers for taking the time to proof read this for me. His insights and suggestions are valuable to me. After the first book was released Brandon, who also writes for The Wrestling Insomniac blog, wrote a very complimentary review of it and I've decided to use it as the forward to this volume. I hope you enjoy reading this book as much as I enjoyed writing these posts. As with the first volume I have updated the chapters as appropriate.

Forward

By Brandon Myers

Last night, I came home from work with one goal in mind: to play as much Dirt 4 as possible. My fiancée is out of town and I had a six uninterrupted hours of video gaming on my schedule. I quickly prepared myself some dinner before plopping down on the couch and booting up my Playstation 4.

While my game was loading, I looked over at my end table and noticed my copy of The Wrestling Insomniac. It was delivered Sunday morning and I took a few minutes to browse through the book, admire the photos and the craftsmanship before placing on it on the table. It had remained there untouched for the past two days and I thought to myself, "I really oughta find some time to read through that." I looked up at the Dirt 4 loading screen and thought about how I had wanted to play some rally cross all day and so I selected my Career Mode to get on with my evening. Then the guilt got to me.

Michael Labbe, founder of this website, is one of my best friends. I know he put a lot of time and effort into crafting this book and I owed it to him to read it sooner rather than later. I set a goal to finish the book by the weekend and I decided I would read it between load screens of my video game.

I read the introduction and then I raced a race. Then I read the first chapter and raced again. The read three chapters and raced again. Then I read three more chapters and raced again.

I should note that my game had fully loaded between all of these reading sessions. I was bombarded by the menu music, but that didn't faze me. I was enthralled with the written word. I couldn't get enough and I just kept reading. I finally pull myself away from the book when I realized I was sick of hearing the same song over and over but after another race I read some more. That's when I decided to turn off my game and the next thing I knew I had read the entire book.

I thought about writing a massive review nitpicking the book and highlighting everything, but I think the story I told above is the best recommendation I can give. If you are visiting the website, you know that Michael is a talented writer. You know that he has an amazing ability to seek out the forgotten history of wrestling and present it in a way that makes you want to learn more. The Wrestling Insomniac is a collection of some of Michael's best blogs first read on TheWrestlingInsomaniac.com. He's added updates for each post and laid out the book so that it's well paced and easy to read.

Reading The Wrestling Insomniac makes you want to go watch wrestling. His chapter on the WWF's big blue cage made me want to watch matches from that era. The breakdown of the history of the NWA World Heavyweight Championship made me want to find those random matches that occurred following the breakup with TNA and before Billy Corgan got involved. The chapter on Goldberg's losses made me want to find a playlist on YouTube with all of them so I could witness them for myself.

The Wrestling Insomniac is a love letter to wrestling. I do not know of a bigger fan of wrestling than Michael Labbe and his passion and love for the sport bleeds out onto the pages of his first book. Am I baised? Definitely, but what you probably don't know is before I wrote for The Wrestling Insomniac I was a fan. It was/is my favorite wrestling site. I enjoyed it so much I felt like I needed to reach out to the creator and express my appreciation. Little did I know that one simple email would lead to me writing for site and the formation of a great friendship. But if it wasn't for the engrossing articles and crazy statistics I would have never sent that

email and the truth is The Wrestling Insomniac (both the book and the website) represent the wrestling stories that I like to read. It's about the forgotten or misremembered wrestling history, the "Oh My God That Actually Happened" moments, and one man's lifelong passion for the squared circle.
So yes, I highly recommend The Wrestling Insomniac get your copy today on Amazon.

First published June 26, 2020

Table of Contents

Photo Log

Cover: Madison Square Garden taken April 6, 2019 at the New Japan Pro Wrestling and Ring of Honor co-promoted G1 Supercard. The first non-WWE wrestling show to be held at the Garden since 1960. My second time at MSG

Page 15: Bret "Hitman" Hart and I at Big Time Wrestling in Augusta, Maine taken March 25, 2012

Page 47: From my signed trading card collection. A Sting card from the 2000 WCW Magazine card set. Signed in person

Page 53: Randy "Macho Man" Savage & Sensational Sherri taken June 4, 1989 WWF at the Cumberland County Civic Center Portland, Maine

Page 90: From my signed trading card collection. United States Champion: Lex Luger cards 92 & 94 from the 1991 Championship Marketing WCW card set. Signed in person at WrestleCon in New York City in April 2019

Page 103: Dan "The Beast" Severn's custom NWA World Heavyweight Championship taken April 5, 2019 in New York City at WrestleCon

Page 176: From my signed card collection. Pedro Morales from the 1991 Wrestling Legends set. Signed by Mr. Morales through the mail.

Page 180: From my signed card collection. Both from the Topps 1985 WWF card set. Greg "The Hammer" Valentine was signed in Person at Supermegafest November 18, 2006 in Framingham, Massachusetts. Tito Santana was signed through the mail.

The Fabulous Freebirds
in the WWE

This was first published on May 16, 2019

The Fabulous Freebirds are one of the greatest wrestling three man teams of all time. There were a few incarnations during their run from 1979 to 1994 with the primary players being Michael P.S. Hayes, Terry "Bam Bam" Gordy, and Buddy Jack Roberts and later in WCW with Jimmy "Jam" Garvin, Badstreet, and others.

In this post we are going to look at the short time that Hayes, Gordy, & Roberts spent in the WWE. Originally brought in to be part of the Rock n' Wrestling Connection, in fact David Wolff is the one that announced that they were coming in. David Wolff was the manager and boyfriend of Cyndi Lauper and Wolff was instrumental in her coming to the WWE and eventually managing Wendi Richter. The Freebirds were to expand this connection and Wolff even appeared at ringside with the Birds.

On The August 4, 1984 episode of Georgia Championship Wrestling taped July 31st at the Mid-Hudson Civic Center in Poughkeepsie, NY David Wolff joined the commentary team of Vince McMahon & Tony Garea where he announced that the Fabulous Freebirds were coming to the WWE

August 4, 1984 Philadelphia Spectrum - Aired 8/19 on GCW: Georgia Championship Wrestling

The Fabulous Freebirds: Michael Hayes, Terry Gordy, & Buddy Roberts with David Wolff & Cyndi Lauper defeated Ron Shaw, Rene Goulet, & Charlie Fulton when Gordy pinned Fulton with a powerbomb

August 10, 1984 Kiel Auditorium, St Louis, Missouri - Aired 8/18 on GCW

The Fabulous Freebirds: Michael Hayes, Terry Gordy, & Buddy Roberts with David Wolff defeated Jerry Valiant, Alexis Smirnoff, & Max Blue when Gordy pinned Valiant

August 25, 1984 Madison Square Garden - Aired 9/8 on GCW

Best 2 out of 3 Falls: The Fabulous Freebirds: Michael Hayes, Terry Gordy, & Buddy Roberts with David Wolff defeated Butcher Vachon, Shaw, & Pete Doherty. Gordy pinned Vachon with a cross body, Robert pinned Doherty with an elbow drop

August 29, 1984 Brantford, Ontario, Canada - Aired 9/29 on Maple Leaf Wrestling

The Fabulous Freebirds: Michael Hayes, Terry Gordy, & Buddy Roberts defeated The Moondogs & Brian Mackney when Gordy pinned Mackney with a piledriver

September 8, 1984 Boston Garden, Massachusetts

The Fabulous Freebirds: Michael Hayes, Terry Gordy, & Buddy Roberts defeated The Moondogs

September 9, 1984 Manchester, New Hampshire

The Fabulous Freebirds: Michael Hayes & Terry Gordy defeated The Moondogs

September 10, 1984 Baltimore, Maryland

The Fabulous Freebirds: Michael Hayes & Terry Gordy defeated The Moondogs

September 11, 1984 Mid-Hudson Civic Center in Poughkeepsie, New York

Aired 9/22 on Championship Wrestling

The Fabulous Freebirds: Michael Hayes, Terry Gordy, & Buddy Roberts with David Wolff & Cyndi Lauper defeated Aldo Marino, Rusty Brooks, & "Iron" Mike Sharpe when Gordy pinned Marino with a piledriver

Aired 10/6 on Championship Wrestling

The Fabulous Freebirds: Michael Hayes, Terry Gordy, & Buddy Roberts with David Wolff defeated Steve Lombardi, Carl Fury, & Bob Orton Jr when Hayes pinned Fury

September 16, 1984 New Haven, Connecticut

The Fabulous Freebirds: Michael Hayes, Terry Gordy, & Buddy Roberts defeated The Moondogs

September 17, 1984 Columbus, Ohio

The Fabulous Freebirds: Michael Hayes, Terry Gordy, & Buddy Roberts defeated The Moondogs

September 18, 1984 Struthers, Ohio

The Fabulous Freebirds: Michael Hayes, Terry Gordy, & Buddy Roberts defeated The Moondogs

September 19, 1984 Erie, Pennsylvania

The Fabulous Freebirds: Michael Hayes, Terry Gordy, & Buddy Roberts defeated The Moondogs

September 22, 1984 Miami, Florida

Michael Hayes defeated Rene Goulet

September 23, 1984 Minneapolis, Minnesota

Michael Hayes & Pat Patterson defeated The Moondogs
This match was advertised as The Freebirds vs. The Moondogs and The Spoiler

September 24, 1984 London, Ontario, Canada - Aired 10/13 on All Star Wrestling

Michael Hayes pinned Dave Barbie

September 28, 1984 Kiel Auditorium, St Louis, Missouri

The Fabulous Freebirds: Michael Hayes, Terry Gordy, & Buddy Roberts defeated The Moondogs by count-out

September 29, 1984 Kansas City, Missouri

The Fabulous Freebirds: Michael Hayes, Terry Gordy, & Buddy Roberts defeated The Moondogs by disqualification

September 30, 1984 Chicago, Illinois

The Fabulous Freebirds: Michael Hayes, Terry Gordy, & Buddy Roberts defeated The Moondogs by count-out

The Freebirds lasted 57 days in the WWE, wrestling 16 matches a unit including debuting at Madison Square Garden. They appeared on four television shows for the promotion, All Star Wrestling, Championship Wrestling, Maple Leaf Wrestling, and Georgia Championship Wrestling.

Rumor has it that the Freebirds left the promotion after Andre "fired" them for showing up late for a show and that Vince McMahon wanted to break the group up. Whatever the reason the Birds didn't last long.

Michael Hayes returned to the WWE in 1995 as Dok Hendrix commentator and backstage interviewer. He eventually started working behind the scenes in various roles still to this day.

Terry Gordy returned to the WWE in November 1996 for a two month run as the masked Executioner including wrestling The Undertaker at In Your House 12 "It's Time" in an Armageddon Rules Match.

On April 2, 2016 The Fabulous Freebirds: Michael Hayes, Terry Gordy, Buddy Roberts, & Jimmy Garvin were inducted in the WWE Hall of Fame.

Update

In the 1986 movie Highlander the titular character Connor MacLeod is seen taking in some wrestling action before he battles another immortal at a nearby parking garage. In the movie it is stated that the wrestling was at Madison Square Garden. Because of this, and the fact that at that time only WWE ran The Garden many assume that this scene was filmed while the Freebirds were in the WWE. This is incorrect.

The match in question was filmed on April 19, 1985 at the Meadowlands in East Rutherford, New Jersey at a joint NWA &

AWA promoted Pro Wrestling USA show. The Fabulous
Freebirds: Michael "PS" Hayes, Terry "Bam Bam" Gordy &
Buddy Jack Roberts wrestled High Flyers: Greg Gagne, & Jim
Brunzell, and The Tonga Kid to a double disqualification

The Final Ride of
Ricky "The Dragon" Steamboat

First published on August 27, 2017

Ricky "The Dragon" Steamboat is one of the greatest wrestlers of all time. A perennial babyface in all the documentaries and interviews I have watched or books I have read I have never heard anyone say anything bad about Steamboat in any way. In fact everyone praises how much they enjoyed wrestling Steamboat and how good he was in the ring.

On August 24, 1994 at Clash of the Champions XXVIII in Cedar Rapids, Iowa Steamboat defeated "Stunning" Steve Austin to win the United States Championship. During the match Steamboat injured his back, he managed to wrestle at house shows the next four days defeating Austin at each one. Unfortunately the injury was too severe and signaled the end of Steamboats in ring career. Or did it?

In the years that followed Steamboat would show up in wrestling in different roles for TNA, Ring of Honor, and various independents, but he never stepped in the ring. In 2005 he returned to the WWE as a road agent. He made it known that he would like to come out of retirement in 2006 at WrestleMania to have a match with Ric Flair, I really wish that that would have happened.

Even though he didn't wrestle Flair he did step back into the ring for the first time in almost 15 years, at WrestleMania XXVI teaming with "Rowdy" Roddy Piper & Jimmy "Superfly" Snuka, losing to Chris Jericho in a three on one handi-capped match.

Steamboat looked amazing! He literally looked like he never lost a step sinking in those deep arm drags, skinning the cat, coming off the top rope, launching himself over the top rope to the floor! Amazing!

The next night on Monday Night Raw, April 6, 2009 in Houston, Texas Steamboat teamed with CM Punk, Jeff Hardy, John Cena, & Rey Mysterio to defeat Jericho, Edge, Kane, Matt Hardy & The Big Show.

On April 26, 2009 at the Backlash pay-per-view in Providence, Rhode Island, Steamboat stepped in the ring with Chris Jericho losing in twelve and a half minutes. Once again Steamboat looked phenomenal in the ring.

In June Steamboat started working select house shows wrestling Sheamus, Drew McIntyre, and Chris Jericho. He won all but his match with Jericho in Japan on July 8, 2009. In August he teamed with his son Richie to defeat Hiram Tua and Orlando Colon at WWC Summer Madness in Puerto Rico.

Steamboat would next compete in the ring on June 18, 2010 once again teaming with Richie at FCW's Father Day Salute in Ft. Myers defeating The Dudebusters. This is Steamboat's last match to date, and it's safe to say it was his last.

No one in wrestling has ever returned to the ring after a 15 year layoff looking as good as Steamboat did. It would have been nice to have seen one of those matches in person or at least released on home video.

The Matches

April 5, 2009 WrestleMania XXVI Houston, Texas

Ricky "The Dragon" Steamboat "Rowdy" Roddy Piper & Jimmy "Superfly" Snuka was defeated by Chris Jericho

April 6, 2009 RAW Houston, Texas

Ricky "The Dragon" Steamboat, CM Punk, Jeff Hardy, John Cena, & Rey Mysterio Jr. defeated Chris Jericho, Edge, Kane, Matt Hardy & The Big Show

April 26, 2009 Backlash Providence, Rhode Island

Ricky "The Dragon" Steamboat defeated by Chris Jericho

June 6, 2009 WWE House Show Pensacola, Florida

Ricky "The Dragon" Steamboat defeated Sheamus

June 13, 2009 WWE House Show Binghamton, New York

Ricky "The Dragon" Steamboat defeated Drew McIntyre

June 14, 2009 WWE House Show Hersey, Pennsylvania

Ricky "The Dragon" Steamboat defeated Drew McIntyre

July 3, 2009 WWE House Show San Diego, California

Ricky "The Dragon" Steamboat defeated Drew McIntyre

July 8, 2009 WWE House Show Tokyo, Japan

Ricky "The Dragon" Steamboat was defeated by Chris Jericho

August 1, 2009 WWE House Show Cape Cod, Massachusetts

Ricky "The Dragon" Steamboat defeated Drew McIntyre

August 2, 2009 WWE House Show Hyannis, Massachusetts

Ricky "The Dragon" Steamboat defeated Drew McIntyre

August 15, 2009 World Wrestling Council, Bayamon, Puerto Rico

Ricky "The Dragon" Steamboat & Richie Steamboat defeated Hiram Tua & Orlando Colon

June 18, 2010 Florida Championship Wrestling, Ft. Myers, Florida

Ricky "The Dragon" Steamboat & Richie Steamboat defeated The Dudebusters: Caylen Croft & Trent Barreta

The Final Run of Bret "Hitman" Hart

First published on June 7, 2018

Growing up I was always a fan of The Hitman, first as part of the Hart Foundation with Jim "The Anvil" Neidhart and later during his singles run. I was sad when he left the WWE even though his departure was one of the most talked about moments in wrestling.

Even though in WCW he won the United States, Tag Team, and World Heavyweight Championships it didn't feel like he did much at all. The injury and abruptness with which his career ended left me feeling like we as fans were cheated. I can't even begin to imagine how Bret felt.

As a fan I wanted to see Bret go out on top, or at least under his own terms, with thunderous applause and not the fizzle that we got. I knew we'd never see him wrestle again, at least that's what I thought, due to the concussion and stroke but it would be nice to see him get the recognition that he deserves.

In 2005 we got our first taste of the return of The Hitman when he worked with the WWE to release a DVD about him: Bret "Hitman" Hart: The Best There Is, The Best There Was, and The Best There Ever Will Be. The documentary was fantastic and the match compilations were great. I was happy that if this was all we got at least it's positive.

Then in 2006 he was the headliner inducted into the WWE Hall of Fame. In his speech he said he was only here for the fans to let them know not to worry about him because he was okay. Once again I thought that this was it, and I was satisfied with this send off as well.

January 4, 2010 was the day that no one ever thought they would see when Bret stepped back into the WWE and faced his old nemesis Shawn Michaels where the two shook hands ending the feud. Later that night a new feud began when Vince McMahon kicked The Hitman in the crotch which led to the unbelievable return of the Hitman to the ring at WrestleMania that year.

That brings us to what this post is about, the final 11 matches of Bret "The Hitman" Hart.

The Matches

March 28, 2010 WrestleMania XXVI Phoenix, Arizona

No Holds Barred: Bret "Hitman" Hart defeated Vince McMahon with special referee Bruce Hart
The match that had to happen! With his family at ringside Hart got his revenge on McMahon after the Montreal Screwjob.

May 17, 2010 RAW, Toronto, Ontario

No Disqualification: Bret "Hitman" Hart submitted United States Champion: The Miz with the sharpshooter to win the championship

August 9, 2010 RAW, Sacramento, California

Lumberjack Match: Bret "Hitman" Hart & John Cena vs. Chris Jericho & Edge went to a no contest

August 15, 2010 SummerSlam Los Angeles, California

Elimination Tag Team Match: Team WWE: Bret "Hitman" Hart, Chris Jericho, Daniel Bryan, Edge, John Cena, John Morrison, & R-Truth defeated Team Nexus: Wade Barrett, Darren Young, David Otunga, Heath Slater, Justin Gabriel, Michael Tarver, & Skip Sheffield

September 25, 2010 SmackDown House Show, Madison Square Garden

Bret "Hitman" Hart and The Hart Dynasty: David Hart Smith & Tyson Kidd with Natayla defeated The Nexus: Heath Slater Justin Gabriel, & Michael Tarver with special guest referee Jerry "The King" Lawler

November 10, 2010 SmackDown House Show Brussel, Belgium

Bret "Hitman" Hart and The Hart Dynasty: David Hart Smith & Tyson Kidd with Natayla defeated The Nexus: Heath Slater, David Otunga, & Husky Harris

November 11, 2010 SmackDown House Show Nuremberg, Germany

Bret "Hitman" Hart and The Hart Dynasty: David Hart Smith & Tyson Kidd with Natayla defeated The Nexus: Heath Slater, Justin Gabriel, & Husky Harris

November 12, 2010 SmackDown House Show Cologne, Germany

Bret "Hitman" Hart and The Hart Dynasty: David Hart Smith & Tyson Kidd with Natayla defeated The Nexus: Heath Slater, David Otunga, & Husky Harris

November 13, 2010 SmackDown House Show Mannheim, Germany

Bret "Hitman" Hart and The Hart Dynasty: David Hart Smith & Tyson Kidd with Natayla defeated The Nexus: David Otunga, Husky Harris, & Justin Gabriel

November 14, 2010 SmackDown House Show İstanbul, Turkey

Bret "Hitman" Hart, Edge, & Rey Mysterio defeated Alberto Del Rio, Cody Rhodes, & Drew McIntyre

September 12, 2011 RAW, Ottawa, Ontario

Bret "Hitman" Hart & John Cena defeated Alberto Del Rio & Ricardo Rodriguez

Over the years going to shows I had the pleasure of seeing Bret live in both matches and an appearance.

June 4, 1989 WWE House Show Portland, Maine

Bret "Hit Man" Hart wrestled Mr. Perfect to a 20 minute time limit draw

August 15, 1995 WWE TV Taping Portland, Maine

Aired 8/26/1995 on Superstars of Wrestling

Bret "Hit Man" Hart submitted Rad Radford with the sharpshooter Jean Pierre Lafitte came to ringside and stole Hart's jacket

Aired on 9/2/1995 Superstars of Wrestling

Bret "Hit Man" Hart defeated Waylon Mercy by disqualification when Jean Pierre Lafitte interfered

Dark Match Bret "Hit Man" Hart defeated Isaac Yankem DDS by count-out

March 1, 1996 WWE House Show Augusta, Maine

Champion: Bret "Hit Man" Hart defeated Undertaker by count-out when Goldust gave Taker a piledriver on the floor

March 25, 2012 Big Time Wrestling in Augusta, Maine.

At this show Bret did a meet and greet and cut a promo in the ring. I got my photo taken with him before the show. This was my Cousin Paul's first live wrestling show in years and Bret is his all-time favorite wrestler. This was a big day for him!

KroniK's Two Week 2001 Run in WWE

First published on August 3, 2017

The WCW tag team KroniK featured two veteran competitors in Brian Adams and Bryan Clark. They were partnered together debuting at Spring Stampede 2000 as hired henchmen of Vince Russo aiding his New Blood stable. They would go on to hold the WCW Tag Team Championships two times totaling 50 days. They were compared to the APA as they too offered protection for a price.

They were in WCW when the promotion was bought by WWE, however they did not immediately join the WWE in the initial influx of WCW talent. They would debut six months later as free agents before eventually joining the WCW/ECW Alliance. Bryan Clark debuted in 1989 in the AWA as the Nightstalker, joining WCW after the AWA folded. At Starrcade he replaced The Diamond Stud, teaming with Rick Steiner losing to Big Van Vader & Mr. Hughes. In 1993 he joined the WWE for a two year run as Adam Bomb where he was initially managed by Harvey Wippleman until he turned face.

He left the WWE in 1995 and from what I can find he didn't return to the ring until he rejoined WCW in 1997 as Wrath in the Blood Runs Cold gimmick. He debuted as a heel joining

Mortis feuding with Glacier and Ernest "The Cat" Miller. He tore his ACL in a match with Jerry Flynn that put him on the shelf for a year where he returned with Brian Adams as KroniK.

Brian Adams debuted for New Japan Pro Wrestling 1986 competing there on and off until 1988. In 1987 he went to the Pacific Northwest territory teaming with The Grappler as The American Ninja. In 1989 he wrestled in the All Japan New Year's Giant Tag Team Series. In the month-long series he would team with Mike Miller, Leo Burke, and Danny Spivey.

In 1990 he debuted in the WWE with an immediate huge push becoming a tag team champion as Crush, the third member of Demolition. After Demolition was disbanded in 1991 he returned as Kona Crush, a Hawaiian surfer babyface. He would turn heel being managed by Mr. Fuji and had a feud with Randy Savage that brought the Macho Man out of retirement for a falls count anywhere match at WrestleMania X.

In 1996 he would change his appearance to that of a biker, still going by Crush he became a member of the Nation of Domination and later the Disciples of Apocalypse. He left the WWE in 1997 and turned up in the WCW as a member of the nWo in 1998 under the name Bryan Adams. In 1998 he was given the gimmick as the KISS Demon making two appearances in the makeup before giving it up to Dale Torborg before ever competing in a match under the gimmick. He finished 1998 competing under his real name before taking a hiatus until the spring of 2000 when he returned as one half of KroniK.

September 10, 2001 Monday Night Raw San Antonio, Texas

KroniK: Brian Adams & Bryan Clark debut attacking the Undertaker putting him through the announce table. They are managed by Steven Richards.
Undertaker was in a match with Booker T when Steven Richards ran in to attack the Undertaker. Taker knocked Richards to the mat and when he bent over to pick him up Booker T nailed an ax-kick getting the pin. Taker then went for the last ride powerbomb on

Richards when KroniK hit the ring.

September 17, 2001 Monday Night Raw Nashville, Tennessee

KroniK: Brian Adams & Bryan Clark with Steven Richards attacked Kane & The Undertaker
WWE & WCW Tag Team Champions: Kane & The Undertaker were wrestling The Dudley Boys: Bubba Ray & D-Von for the WWE Tag Team Championships. The ref was bumped and Kane was about to chokeslam Bubba Ray through a table on the floor when KroniK ran in and double chokeslammed Kane through the table. They then went after the Undertaker causing a distraction that led to a 3D on The Deadman and the three count crowning new WWE Tag Team Champions.
When Shane arrived at the building KroniK & Steven Richard approached Kane offering their services to the Alliance, which Shane accepted and then booked them in a match at Unforgiven for the WCW Tag Team Titles.

September 18, 2001 Smackdown Memphis, Tennessee

KroniK: Brian Adams & Bryan Clark with Steven Richards defeat Kientai: Taka Michinoku & Sho Funaki
In their in-ring debut they easily defeated the Japanese tag team and won with a double chokeslam on Taka. In WCW the finish was called High Times but in WWE they just called it a double chokeslam.

September 22, 2001 House Show, Reading, Pennsylvania

Kane & Albert defeated Kronik: Brian Adams & Bryan Clark
Albert substituted for The Undertaker in this match. Kane pinned Bryan Clark after a chokeslam. This would be KroniK's only house show appearance.

September 23, 2001 Unforgiven, Pittsburgh, Pennsylvania

WCW Tag Team Champions: Kane & The Undertaker defeated
KroniK: Brian Adams & Bryan Clark with Steven Richards
This was an ok back and forth match, I wouldn't call either tag
team dominant. The finish came after a chokeslam on Clark by
The Undertaker.

This was the last appearance for KroniK in the WWE. I'm
not sure why they left the WWE it seems like everything ended
just as it got started. They would wrestle for the Heartland
Wrestling Association in Ohio in October and November 2001.
In February 2002 they appeared on the WWA Pay-Per-
View in Las Vegas defeating Ghostwalker and Navajo Warrior.
That July they debuted for All Japan Pro Wrestling and defeated
Keiji Muto & Taiyo Kea for the AJPW Tag Team Championships.
They were stripped of the titles for failing to defend them. Their
last match together as a tag team came on January 19, 2003 in
Tokyo, Japan for Wrestle-1 losing to Keiji Muto & Bill Goldberg.

The Abysmal WWE Run of "Dr. Death" Steve Williams

First published on July 20, 2018

When I was a kid I was a big fan of "Dr. Death" Steve Williams. Admittedly it was initially probably his moniker that made me pay attention to him. Ultimately it was his in ring work that made me a fan.

I first saw him in Jim Crockett Promotions as a member of the Varsity Club and he was such a monster I just couldn't get enough. He returned in 1992 with Terry Gordy as the Miracle Violence Connection, dominating the tag team division, eventually becoming the NWA/WCW Unified Tag Team Champions. Their 30 minute time limit draw with the Steiner Brothers at Beach Blast 1992 was tremendous!

Today wrestling from around the world is a lot more accessible than in the 1980's & 90's, so when Williams had that tremendous run in All Japan I was relegated to reading about it in the magazines and through the occasional tape I was able to get my hands on.

When it was announced that he had signed with the WWE I couldn't have been more excited. He had a dark match in April of 1998 but his in ring debuted didn't until July and it wasn't in a wrestling match but in infamous Brawl for All where in the second round he was knock out by Bart Gunn and in the progress tore his hamstring and other injuries that kept him out of action for months. He returned in January 1999 defeating Bob Holly in a dark match. We next saw him on television dressed in a kabuki outfit with a mask. It was Raw that aired February 22, 1999, taped on the 16th, when during a hardcore match between Bart Gunn and Bob Holly when Kabuki ran out throwing Gunn off the stage through a table.

Jim Ross suffered a Bell's Palsy attack that took him off air. When he returned he was a disgruntled heel that was bitter about losing his spot and he began acting as a manager for Doctor Death upon his return from injury.

On the March 14th episode of Sunday Night Heat Tiger Ali Singh brought a fan into the ring to do an imitation of Ross. Ross and Williams came down the ring and Williams suplexed the fan on the back of his head.

Ironically the fan was WWE writer Ed Ferrara who would go onto the WCW later in 1999 and play a character named Oklahoma that spoofed Jim Ross and acted the manager of Williams during his abysmal WCW run in 1999.

Williams would wrestle in only three matches in March of 1999 before being released in mid-April. In his year in the WWE Williams wrestled five matches and competed in two Brawl for All bouts. He was involved in a couple minor feuds with Tiger Ali Singh, Bob Holly and Al Snow but he made no impact at all in the WWE.

As a fan I was disappointed and I have to imagine that Dr. Death was as well. He would return to the WWE in late May 2003 wrestling two house shows against Lance Storm in Louisiana.

The Matches

April 28, 1998 Dark Match Richmond, Virginia

"Dr Death" Steve Williams pinned Too Cold Scorpio with a backdrop driver

July 14, 1998 RAW Birmingham, New York

Brawl 4 All: "Dr Death" Steve Williams defeated Pierre Carl Ouellet by decision in three rounds

July 27, 1998 RAW Anaheim, California

Brawl 4 All: Bart Gunn knockout "Dr Death" Steve Williams in the third round

January 12, 1999 Dark Match Beaumont, Texas

"Dr Death" Steve Williams defeated Bob Holly

March 15, 1999 Sunday Night Heat San Jose, California

"Dr Death" Steve Williams defeated Matt & Jeff Hardy in a handicapped match with an Oklahoma Stampede on Matt

March 29, 1999 RAW East Rutherford, New Jersey

Hardcore Champion: Hardcore Holly defeated "Dr Death" Steve Williams after Al Snow interfered to retain his championship

March 30, 1999 Sunday Night Heat Nassau Coliseum

"Dr Death" Steve Williams defeated Tiger Ali Singh

May 23, 2003 House Show Bossier City, Louisiana

"Dr Death" Steve Williams defeats Lance Storm

May 24, 2003 House Show Baton Rouge, Louisiana

Lance Storm defeated "Dr Death" Steve Williams

"Dr. Death" Steve Williams 1999 run in WCW

First published April 15, 2020

A couple years ago I wrote a post about Dr. Death's Abysmal WWE Run. After he left the WWE in March of 1999 he wrestled a single match in All Japan Pro Wrestling at the Giant Baba Memorial Show before he turned up in World Championship Wrestling.

Monday Nitro November 15, 1999 Little Rock, Arkansas

"Dr. Death" Steve Williams WCW debut. Williams was shown walking into the arena Ed Ferrara who was doing his Jim Ross impersonation and going by the name Oklahoma. Later that night Williams and Oklahoma joined the commentary team during a Pinata on a Pole Match. Eventually Williams interrupted the match, laying out Silver King, El Dandy, Psychosis, Juventude, and the Villanos. Inside the pinata was a $10,000 check that Williams claimed for himself after Silver King had retrieved it.

Monday Nitro November 29, 1999 Denver, Colorado

Steel Cage: "Dr. Death" Steve Williams vs. Jerry Only

That's right, Williams' first official match in WCW was a Steel Cage match against the lead singer for the band Misfits, and he lost. I'm a fan of the Misfits, they've got some great tunes. At this time they were teamed up with Vampiro, but there is no reason why this match happened. Doc dominated the entire match and the finish came when he threw Only into the corner by the cage door and Only fell to the floor to win by escaping the cage.

Thunder December 2, 1999 Topeka, Kansas

3 on 1 Handicapped Match: "Dr. Death" Steve Williams vs. Silver King, Villano IV & V
While Doc was dominating the Luchadors, Vampiro and the Misfits jumped Oklahoma on the floor. You would think this would lead to him getting distracted and pinned or he would defend Oklahoma and win by disqualification. Nope, Doc pinned one of the Villanos clean in the center of the ring after an Oklahoma Stampede. The real story out of this was that Silver King managed to retrieve the $10,000 check back from Oklahoma and ran off with it. Seems odd to still be carrying that check around over two weeks later and not have deposited or cashed it.

Monday Nitro December 6, 1999 Milwaukee, Wisconsin

"Dr. Death" Steve Williams & Oklahoma vs. Vampiro & Jerry Only
Oklahoma wore a microphone and called the action during the match. Doc dominated, Oklahoma got beat up for a spell. Then Doc got Vampiro down with the Stampede and Oklahoma got the pin for his team.

Monday Nitro December 13, 1999 New Orleans, Louisiana

"Dr. Death" Steve Williams vs. Sid
This was billed as a Powerbomb vs. Suplex match that Williams lost in two and a half minutes. Such a friggin disgrace. Williams

was huge in the Mid-South region and in New Orleans and he lost in short order in a crap gimmick match.

Thunder December 16, 1999 Mobile, Alabama

"Dr. Death" Steve Williams vs. The Wall
Doc won this match by DQ when Berlyn aka Alex Wright hit Williams with his cane, something he attempted to do behind the referee's back but failed. Doc and The Wall beat the tar out of each other for a couple minutes then the DQ. This match was more about The Wall and Berlyn breaking up than getting Doc over.

Starrcade December 19, 1999 Washington D.C.

"Dr. Death" Steve Williams vs. Vampiro
This match had a couple stipulations including Oklahoma in a cage above the ring and if Vampiro won he'd get five minutes in the ring with Oklahoma. Doc lost this by DQ in just under five minutes which granted Vampiro 5 minutes with Oklahoma. Security removed Doc from the ringside area and Oklahoma got destroyed.

This was the last match that Williams had in WCW. In total his run lasted 24 days, he wrestled six matches winning three and losing three primarily feuding with Vampiro and the Misfits. Not a single match in this run went over five minutes. It was uneventful and a sad closure to Doc's major US coverage.

He would spend the next three years wrestling full time for All Japan Pro Wrestling. In 2003 he wrestled a couple house show matches against Lance Storm in the WWE, had a program with MLW competing in a War Games match.

Sadly in 2004 he was diagnosed with throat cancer and underwent surgery. He was cancer free in 2005 and returned to wrestling competing on the indies. In 2007 he helped do some training in OVW, even tagging with fellow Oklahoman Jake Hager for a couple tag team matches. I think this explains why Hager uses the Doctor Bomb.

Williams retired from wrestling in 2008 and in 2009 his cancer returned. He passed away on December 29, 2009 at the age of 49.

Chris Candido's
Three Months in WCW

First published May 13, 2017

Chris Candido passed away just over twelve years ago on April 28, 2005 from pneumonia. He had broken his leg in a match just a few days before and had to have surgery to repair his tibia and fibula.

Originally it was reported that a blot clot from the surgery caused his death but his brother has since stated otherwise. There has been much written about Chris's career but in this post I'm going to focus only on his time in World Championship Wrestling. Candido debuted March 19, 2000 in Miami, Florida at WCW Uncensored on commentary during the Cruiserweight Championship match between champion The Artist and Psychosis.

He made his in-ring debut the next night March 20th on Monday Nitro from Gainesville, Florida defeating Lash LaRoux with a headbutt off the top rope. The night after that he lost to Chavo Guerrero on Thunday, so he wasn't off to a big start. He would avenge his loss to Chavo, beating him on Thunder March 29, 2000 and was on the losing end of a six man tag match on the Thunder prior to Spring Stampede.

At Spring Stampede, April 16th from the United Center in Chicago, Candido would capture the vacant Cruiserweight

Championship defeating Shane Helms, Shannon Moore, Crowbar, Lash Laroux, The Artist, & Juventud Guerrera. Tammy Sytch joined Chris this night making a run-in pushing The Artist off the top rope. After the match Sytch and Paisley fought until they were pulled apart.

Candido & Sytch would team together to defeat The Artist and Paisley at Monday Nitro from Rochester, New York on April 24th. Candido would retain the title over the next few weeks in matches against The Artist and Crowbar. Candido would lose the title at the May 15th Nitro from Biloxi, Mississippi in a Mixed Tag match teaming with Tammy in a loss to Crowbar and Daffney who became co-champions.

On Thunder May 30th in Boise, Idaho, aired May 31st, Chris Candido wrestled Hardcore Champion: Terry Funk in what is my favorite match of his WCW run. Candido comes to the ring first dressed and acting like Terry Funk. He then meets Funk on the entrance ramp, attacking him about halfway to the ring; this was the closest the match got to the ring.

The action quickly spread to the back and out to the parking lot where Funk threw Candido in the back of a pick-up and then sped off across the parking lot with the referee chasing them on foot. They end up down the road from the area a short distance at a horse stable. There they commence to fighting including a spot where Candido drives Funk's into a pile of horse dung.

They spill into a horse stall where Funk piledrives Candido and a very unimpressed horse kicks both of them. For reasons never explained a standard "wrestling" table is present, Candido sets Funk on it and begins to climb the stall, Funk pulls Candido off through the table. The referee finally catches up and for reasons unknown Funk hits the ref with a trash can knocking him out. He then attempts a pinfall but there is no one to count it. Funk dumps a bucket of water on the official, reviving him and then pinned Candido for the win.My only issue with this match is the fact that a camera crew was already at the stable instead of chasing them down there.

The remainder of Candido's run was uneventful. He, Shane

Douglas, and Bam Bam Bigelow reformed the Triple Threat for a few weeks before Candido departed. His final match in WCW was taped on June 20th in Bozeman, Montana for Thunder, aired June 21th, where he and Bigelow defeated Buff Bagwell in a handicapped match.

To summarize he was in WCW for only 93 days, he competed in 21 matches, losing twelve winning 9, he was the Cruiserweight Champion for 29 days, he wrestled matches on Nitro, Thunder, Worldwide and two house shows, and he made appearances at three Pay-Per-Views, Uncensored, Spring Stampede, & Slamboree, wrestling at two of them.

Candido started training at the age of 14 and was only 33 years old when he died. I cannot imagine what he could have accomplished in his career had he not passed away.

The Ultimate Warrior's WCW Run

First published on July 1, 2017

In 1998 The Ultimate Warrior returned to the wrestling world after a two plus year hiatus from the ring, this time though it was in World Championship Wrestling. Since 1987, The Ultimate Warrior had made his home in the World Wrestling Federation but he had not been since a dark match at a Superstars television taping June 25, 1996 when he defeated Vader by count-out.

On Monday August 17, 1998 from Hartford, Connecticut WCW presented Monday Nitro. About halfway through the show Hogan was in the ring for his second promo of the night. He was talking about how there was no one that could beat him.

After he uttered the line "There's not a warrior I can't beat to get my belt back" the arena lights started to flicker on and off before shutting off. Then a voice could be heard and some odd music started that included thunder and lightning effects. As the man walked to the ring you couldn't see who it was at all, then they cut to Hogan who was standing there with his mouth hanging open. When they cut back you could finally see it was the Ultimate Warrior.

Warrior entered the ring to a tremendous pop from the crowd who chanted "Warrior!" He then rambled on the mic for just over 12 minutes basically saying I beat you before, I'm not here to beat you because everyone has, I'll see you next week. The rest was just nonsense. The ring filled with smoke, the lights flickered and he disappeared. The final shot was a Warrior style bat signal shining in the arena. Total segment time was 19 minutes.

The Warrior would continue to appear on Nitro leading up to his first match in WCW at Fall Brawl 98:

August 24, 1998 Monday Nitro Chicago, IL

Warrior's music has been changed up this week, the same slow heavy metal opening and then it switched to a fast-paced music similar to his WWE theme to which he charges the ring and enters in the fashion we are used to. This promo lasts about ten minutes where basically he says, Hogan was a good guy and now he's a bad guy, but in Warrior's own unique vernacular. Also he introduces the One Warrior Nation.

August 31, 1998 Monday Nitro Miami, FL

Hogan comes out for a promo and Warrior interrupts Hogan, then almost immediately after he enters the ring he makes his smoky exit. They show Warrior in the rafters through-out the show. At the end of the show Hogan is in the ring, the ring fills with smoke and the Warrior returns and Hogan runs away.

September 7, 1998 Monday Nitro Pensacola, FL

Hogan opens the show with a promo saying you'll have to get through the Disciple to get to me. Through-out the show members of the nWo kept being laid out with the Warriors mark being left. In the closing segment Hogan is in the ring with The Giant, they lower a steel cage. Hogan says if Warrior can beat The Giant then he deserves a match with Hogan. The ring fills with smoke and when it settles Warrior is in the cage sitting on a chair with The

Giant unconscious on the mat. Warrior misses a chair shot, Hogan connects to Warriors back and he no sells it. Hogan runs out of the ring locking the cage door. The ring fills with smoke and Warrior disappears closing the show.

September 13, 1998 Fall Brawl 98 Winston-Salem, SC

This was the absolute worst ever War Games match and sadly it was the last. Instead of two teams competing against each other until all competitors are in the ring and then the finish comes when someone submits or surrenders, there were three teams. In the first five minute segment the match could end if either Bret Hart or DDP scored a fall on the other. Also for the first time ever there was a referee in the ring as pinfalls counted.
After the first five minute segment a random member of another team would enter every two minutes until all competitors were in the ring and then it was first fall. Team WCW: DDP, Roddy Piper, & Warrior, Team nWo Hollywood: Hogan, Stevie Ray, & Bret Hart, and Team nWo Wolfpac: Kevin Nash, Sting, & Lex Luger. Hogan was the second to last to enter, which he did over a minute early. He and Stevie Ray took out everyone with a slapjack, including teammate Bret Hart. Hogan went for the pin on Kevin Nash when the ring filled with smoke, Warrior appeared in the ring pounding his chest, he was attacked from behind and crumbled to the canvas. The ring filled with smoke again and when it cleared Hogan was holding his jacket. Warrior that ran down the entrance way going after Hogan and Stevie Ray. Hogan left the ring locking the cage as Stevie Ray was taken out by Warrior.
Warrior then walked around the ring stalking Hogan as he circled the outside of the ring. Warrior kicked an opening in the cage chasing after Hogan where security separated them in the aisle!?! Seriously!
Back to the ring where everyone has been on the mat for now over five minutes, Stevie Ray and DDP get up, Ray eats a Diamond Cutter and Page gets the win. Completely bullshit garbage!

September 14, 1998 Monday Nitro Greenville, South Carolina

This episode of Nitro featured the greatest segment in the history
of Nitro, the return of "Nature Boy" Ric Flair. I remember
watching this live and I had tears in my eyes. But this is about The
Ultimate Warrior. Hogan was in the ring with Bischoff, Miss.
Elizabeth, & The Disciple and cuts a promo challenging the
Warrior to a match at Halloween Havoc because he's angry that
Warrior cost him the match last night at Fall Brawl. Smoke filled
the ring and when it cleared The Disciple was gone. Warrior never
actually appeared on the show.

September 21, 1998 Monday Nitro Boston, Massachusetts

Show opens with the smoke filling with smoke and The Disciple is
face down in the center of the ring. Hogan and the nWo come out,
ring fills with smoke again and The Disciple is gone. Show ends
with Hogan in the ring, Warrior comes out followed by the
Disciple who has joined the One Warrior Nation.

September 28, 1998 Monday Nitro Rochester, New York

The Disciple came out for a match representing the One Warrior
Nation to the nWo's entrance music, sure that makes sense.
Warrior came out for a promo a fan try to get in the ring and
security caught him before he got to his feet but it was caught on
camera. He rambled for a long time and I think he accepted
Hogan's challenge for a match at Halloween Havoc.

October 5, 1998 Monday Nitro Columbia, South Carolina

They aired what I'm guessing was a pre-taped segment of the
Warrior cutting a promo, I have no idea what he said other than
"Feel the power of the Warrior!"

October 12, 1998 Monday Nitro Chicago, Illinois

Sting came out to cut a promo on Bret Hart and Hulk Hogan, Warrior came out and took a long time to say if Sting is calling out the anti-heroes then allow us to stand side by side. Translated, that means that later Blade Runners will reunite to take on Hogan and Hart.

This was a treat actually because I don't remember at all this match happening. After some stalling Hogan and Sting start, Hogan takes a beating and then tags in Hart. Hart takes a beating until Hogan comes in, with the referee distracted by the Warrior, Hart hits Sting with a low blow. Sting takes a beating from Hart, then Hogan tags in and continues on the offense.

Hart tags in continuing to work over Sting until he misses an elbow drop off the second rope. Sting tags in Warrior who is apparently going to wrestle in his trench coat and jeans. Warrior hits Hart with three clotheslines and signals for the press slam, Hogan hits Warrior from behind. The nWo black and white runs in causing the disqualification.

The ring fills with smoke so they throw Warrior to the outside so he can't disappear., makes sense. Sting attacks the nWo with the baseball bat, Warrior gets Hogan's weight belt and chases them to the back, whipping them all as they go off the air. Match was about 5 minutes long and not all that good.

October 19, 1998 Monday Nitro Minneapolis, Minnesota

Hollywood Hogan brings Horace out to the ring revealing that Horace is his nephew the rest of the nWo comes out, looks like he's going to join the nWo, SWERVE!! Hogan attacks Horace, then whips him with his belt, basically he says if I would do this to someone I love, imagine what I'll do to you. Hogan then brained Horace with a chair busting him open.

Warrior hits the ring to make the save, in actual wrestling gear. Hogan flees the ring as Warrior cleans house with a baseball bat. The Giant manages the hit Warrior from behind then plants him with a choke slam. Hogan then spray paints Warrior and nails two leg drops. Typically when you're going into the PPV the guy standing tall loses the match, not in this case.

October 25, 1998 Halloween Havoc Las Vegas, Nevada

Surprisingly this match opens with both men working the arm before Hogan takes a powder to slow it down. These guys did a test of strength, criss cross, traded body slams and spilled to the floor in the first few minutes.
Then an accidental referee bump, then Hogan dropped two knees on Nick Patrick. The Giant comes out, Hogan holds Warrior but he ducks and The Giant levels Hogan. Warrior then clears The Giant out of the ring. Nick Patrick comes too just in time to watch Hogan hit Warrior directly on the side of the head with his weight belt. Which looked wicked vicious!
Eventually Warrior returns the favor with the weight belt. Hogan tries to throw a fireball in Warriors face, but it malfunctions and it doesn't work. Hogan is busted open but I watched and re-watched and can't see what busted him open. Hogan hits Warrior in the balls right in front of the referee.
Horace comes to the ring with a chair, I guess he's looking for revenge on Uncle Terry. Bischoff jumps on the apron and puts Nick Patrick in a front face lock, Horace gets in the ring and cracks Warrior over the back of the head with the chair. Hogan with the cover and a handful of tights and that's good for the three count. Terrible, just terrible. Incidentally this is not billed as a no-disqualification match and yet I counted at least a half dozen times when a disqualification should have been called for.
Post match Hogan tells Horace that he passed the test and that he loved him. Horace then starts spraying Warrior with liquid from a lighter fluid bottle. Doug Dillinger jumps in the ring and takes the lighter away from Hogan. With nothing to set the Warrior a blaze they leave. Terrible.

October 26, 1998 Monday Nitro Phoenix, Arizona

Warrior comes out to the ring and cuts a promo on Hogan about their match at Halloween Havoc. Basically in translated Warrior speak he said that Hogan took the cheap way out, that he beat the hell out of Hogan. He also said that the bullshit pinfall means nothing. Hogan comes out to go after the Warrior, Horace and Bischoff talk him out of it. Horace eats a few clotheslines before being sent over the top rope. The Giant then enters but is also clotheslined out of the ring. Hogan attacks from behind but Warrior reverses with this flying shoulder tackle. Warrior then strikes Eric Bischoff. The nWo retreat.

November 9, 1998 Monday Nitro Long Island, New York

The Disciple is in the ring saying he's not with the nWo that he's his own man and he's not watching Hogan's back anymore. Horace, Stevie Ray, & Vincent hit the ring where Horace cut a promo about him turning his back on Hogan. They attacked the Disciple beating him down. Warrior hits the ring making the save and they cut to commercial break during this segment.

This is the last time we see Warrior on WCW television. In interviews later on Warrior would say the only reason he was brought into WCW was for Hogan to get a win over Warrior making up for his loss at WrestleMania VI.

The Ultimate Warrior was in World Championship Wrestling for 77 days, appearing on eleven Monday Nitros and two Pay Per Views. He wrestled in three matches, a three team nine man match, a tag team match on Nitro, and a singles match.

This post is the least enjoyable one that I have ever researched for this blog. When I started down this road I thought it would be fun but the more I got into it did I find out that I was very wrong. It became a chore to listen to the promos and watch the matches. UGH!!

Rick Martel's WCW 1998 Run

First published on July 20, 2017

At the beginning of 1998 Rick Martel hadn't competed regularly in wrestling since 1994. The former three-time WWE Tag Team Champion and AWA World Heavyweight Champion had been a mainstay in the WWE since 1986 however, he made only two appearances in 1995. First, he competed in the 1995 Royal Rumble, and the second an appearance in a non-wrestling babyface role at the Montreal Forum on February 3rd.

Growing up to me Martel was a WWE guy, needless to say I was shocked to see him jog out to the ring on the January 5, 1998 Monday Nitro to take on Brad Armstrong. Since that time I have learned, most recently when Don talked about it on Killing the Town, that Don Callis and Rick Martel were gearing up to wrestle as a tag team in the WWE as the Supermodels.

Martel and Callis even had several matches as a team in the IWA in Canada against Christian Cage & Rhino and Adam Impact & Christian Cage. I'm sure you know who they are today. However, at the last minute Martel either reached out to or was contacted by WCW and he ended up there for his only run in the promotion.

January 5, 1998 WCW Nitro Georgia Dome, Atlanta

Rick Martel defeated Brad Armstrong
In this match, Armstrong, the Georgia native lasted only about five minutes before submitting to the Quebec Crab. It was odd to me that Armstrong was the heel in this match as he's in his home state

and had been a longtime babyface in this promotion against a guy who had never wrestled in WCW before and was a longtime heel.

January 6, 1998 WCW Saturday Night taping Rome, Georgia

Aired January 10, 1998

Rick Martel defeated Mark Truian with the Quebec Crab in about four minutes
Backstage interview with Martel about his arrival in WCW. This promo is on YouTube and it's pretty generic, "I'm here because this company is the best in the world, and I plan on challenging for championships."

Aired January 17, 1998

Rick Martel defeated Hardbody Harrison with the Quebec Crab in about four minutes
This match is on YouTube, Martel was dominant working the legs until he applied his finisher for the submission. During Martel's entrance, footage from the January 12th Nitro was shown of Martel helping Booker T.

January 8, 1998 WCW Thunder Daytona Beach, Florida

Rick Martel defeated Louie Spicolli with the Quebec Crab just under three and a half minutes

January 12, 1998 WCW Monday Nitro Jacksonville, Florida

During the Booker T vs. Saturn match for Booker's World Television Championship Saturn cheated to win, Martel ran down getting the referee to restart the match where Booker T retained his title. Martel told Booker that he owed him one.

January 19, 1998 WCW Monday Nitro, Superdome New Orleans, Louisiana

Rick Martel defeated Eddie Guerrero with the Quebec Crab in just over five minutes.
Guerrero jumped Martel as he entered the ring. Martel fired back taking the offensive even hitting a gorilla press slam, something I don't think I've ever seen Martel do! A really good match, Guerrero was so good and he was able to fit so much into this short match without doing too much. Martel hit a spine buster holding onto the legs he turned it right over into his finish. The crowd was hot!
Later in the show after Booker T defeated Mortis to defend his Television Championship Mortis attacked him. Martel made the save and Booker T agreed to defend the Television Championship against him at Souled Out.

January 20, 1998 WCW Saturday Night taping Thibodaux, Louisiana

Aired January 24, 1998

Rick Martel defeated Johnny Attitude with the Quebec Crab in just over two minutes. Footage was shown of the attack from the January 22nd Thunder.
A promo aired of Martel talking about his match later tonight against Booker T for the World Television Championship at Souled Out. That's right, Martel wrestled in a taped match on Wednesday that aired the same night as his PPV match. Why would they have him wrestle on the taped Saturday Night and the Live PPV, I just don't get that.

January 22, 1998 WCW Thunder Huntsville, Alabama

Rick Martel defeated Perry Saturn with the Quebec Crab

I found this match on YouTube, it's a decent back and forth match until Martel rolls through a sunset flip to lock in his finisher for the submission. When Martel arrived at the building Kidman and Perry Saturn attacked Martel throwing him through a glass door.

January 24, 1998 WCW Souled Out, Dayton, Ohio

World Television Champion: Booker T defeated Rick Martel

January 29, 1998 WCW Thunder, Mid-South Coliseum, Memphis, Tennessee

World Television Champion: Booker T defeated Saturn, during the match Lodi, Billy Kidman, Sick Boy, & Riggs attempted to interfere and Martel ran out preventing them. After the match Booker T and Martel had words with each other.

February 14, 1998 WCW Worldwide, Universal Studios, Florida

Rick Martel defeated Barry Houston with the Quebec Crab in about three minutes
I found this match on YouTube, it's not listed on any of my typical sources for results. However this was taped during the days when taping several weeks of matches at once.

February 16, 1998 WCW Monday Nitro, Tampa, Florida

Perry Saturn defeated Rick Martel with the Rings of Saturn
The match was supposed to be Saturn vs. Disco Inferno, on the way to the ring La Parka attacked Disco, laying him out with a chair. For reasons I can't understand Martel came out and challenged Saturn. It was a very good match that ended when the Kidman distracted the referee and Riggs attacked Martel.

Rick Martel submitted World Television Champion: Booker T

with the Quebec Crab to win the championship.

That's right, two matches later Martel returned to the ring to capture his first and only WCW championship. After the ref was bumped, Saturn attempted to interfere which led to Booker hitting Saturn with a spin kick that injured his knee, leading to the submission win for Martel. In another odd moment Martel worked as babyface against Saturn earlier but was a heel here against Booker T.

February 22, 1998 WCW SuperBrawl VIII Cow Palace, San Francisco, California

Booker T defeated World Television Champion: Rick Martel
This was a very good match. I couldn't see where Martel injured himself and I was looking for it. This was probably the best match of his WCW run. This was a gauntlet match that Martel was supposed to win facing Saturn after Booker T. Because of the injury Martel dropped the title to Booker who went on to also defeat Saturn.

July 13, 1998 WCW Monday Nitro, Las Vegas, Nevada

Stevie Ray defeated Rick Martel after a slapjack
Martel had Stevie Ray in the Quebec Crab when Bret Hart ran out and hit Martel in the back of the head with a chair, the ref didn't see it. Ray then hit his finish, the slapjack, which is his variation of the pedigree.

If you watch it Martel lands on the crown of his head and according to his RF Shoot Interview it injured two vertebrae in his neck. He said he was hesitant to take the move because he didn't want to land on his knee after just having surgery. Martel said that was enough for him and he hung up the boots.

After being injured again in his first match back Martel retired from the ring working for WCW as a trainer and working as a host for the French versions of their show. Incidentally his entrance music in WCW was terrible. Martel would wrestle one more match on March 20, 1999 in Hawaii defeating The Metal Maniac for Hawaiian International Wrestling Federation.

Martel is one of only a few men to hold a championship in the AWA, WWE, and WCW. He also held championships in Stampede Wrestling and various NWA promotions. Had he not been injured I suspect he would still have finished his career in WCW just not the way he did.

Martel spent 189 days in WCW, 141 out with injury; he wrestled at least twelve matches, appearing on two Pay-Per-Views, Nitro, Thunder, Saturday Night and syndicated programming. He held the WCW World Television Championship for six days.

The Second WCW Run of The Public Enemy

First published on August 21, 2017

Many people are well aware of the tag team The Public Enemy: "Flyboy" Rocco Rock & Johnny Grunge. They helped revolutionize the early days of ECW, becoming four time tag team champions from September 18, 1993 to January 5, 1996. They jumped to WCW in January 1996 to September 1998 winning the WCW world tag team championships.

In 1999 the team returned to the land of the extreme, wrestling The Dudley Boys to a no contest at House Party 99 on January 16th at the ECW arena. They were supposed to make more appearances in ECW but cancelled them when they signed with the WWE for their disastrous run in that promotion.

Many fans, myself included, forget that the duo made a return to World Championship Wrestling in the summer of 1999 at Bash of the Beach pay-per-view and exiting just over a month later.

June 25, 1999 House Show Auburn Hills, Michigan

Hak defeated Johnny Grunge in a hardcore match
I was surprised to learn about this house show match and wish I

could find more about it.

July 11, 1999 Bash at the Beach Ft. Lauderdale, Florida

Competed in a Hardcore Junkyard Invitational that was won by Fit Finlay. This was the team's surprise return to WCW after a ten month absence.

August 3, 1999 WCW Saturday Night, Mankato, Minnesota

The Public Enemy: "Flyboy" Rocco Rock and Johnny Grunge defeated Hugh Morrus & Jerry Flynn by disqualification

August 5, 1999 Thunder Lacrosse, Wisconsin

Goldberg pinned "Flyboy" Rocco Rock

August 9, 1999 Monday Nitro Boise, Idaho

West Texas Rednecks: Curt Hennig & Barry Windham defeated The Public Enemy: "Flyboy" Rocco Rock and Johnny Grunge

August 16, 1999 Monday Nitro Colorado Springs, Colorado

The Insane Clown Posse: Violent Jay & Shaggy 2 Dope defeated The Public Enemy: "Flyboy" Rocco Rock and Johnny Grunge

August 17, 1999 WCW Saturday Night, Casper, Wyoming

The Public Enemy: "Flyboy" Rocco Rock and Johnny Grunge defeated nWo: Scott Norton & Horace

August 18, 1999 House Show Amarillo, Texas

Chris Benoit & Perry Saturn defeated The Public Enemy: "Flyboy" Rocco Rock and Johnny Grunge

August 19, 1999 Thunder, Lubbock, Texas - Aired August 26

Sid Vicious defeated The Public Enemy: "Flyboy" Rocco Rock and Johnny Grunge in a handicapped match

1999 was an interesting year for The Public Enemy. They started the year in ECW, had a brief run in WWE, held the NWA World Tag Team Championships for two days in June, returned to WCW in July and August, and finished the year working for the California based XPW.

Sadly both members of the team have since passed away, Rocco Rock in 2002 and Johnny Grunge in 2006. I was always a fan of them, in-fact they main evented the first ever indie show that I went to. On March 16, 1997 at Edward Little High School in Auburn, Maine, they defeated Dave and Dean the Power Twins with the Drive By through a table. My buddy Jay actually brought home half the table as a souvenir.

Sting's Lost WCW Matches

First published September 14, 2018

I'm sure anyone reading this book knows who Sting is and I don't need to explain who he is. Many people recall back in 1996 the build to Fall Brawl War Games the nWo led us to believe that Sting had turned on WCW and joined them. They even had a fake Sting, Jeff Farmer, to try and fool the WCW faithful.

Sting was the last competitor to enter the War Games cage that night and when Lex still didn't believe Sting he walked out, changing his appearance eventually becoming the Crow Sting that hung out in the rafters for over a year until finally challenging Hollywood Hogan for the World Championship at Starrcade 1997.

Most people, myself included, didn't think Sting competed in the ring at all during that time frame. I was surprised to learn recently that he did wrestle several matches during that time. Four days after Fall Brawl he went to Japan for a four show tour with New Japan Pro Wrestling.

September 19, 1996 Okayama, Japan

Sting defeated Masahiro Chono

September 20, 1996 Osaka, Japan

Sting & Shiro Koshinaka defeated Ookami Gundan: Hiro Saito & Masahiro Chono

September 21, 1996 Korakuen Hall, Tokyo, Japan

Shiro Koshinaka defeated Sting

September 23, 1996 Yokohama, Japan

"Total Package" Lex Luger & Sting defeated "Enforcer" Arn Anderson & "Lord" Steven Regal
This match is hilarious to me because the whole reason Sting walked out on WCW at Fall Brawl is because his best friend Lex Luger didn't believe in him.

He then worked a series of house show matches with WCW.

October 6, 1996 North Charleston, South Carolina

The Giant defeated "Macho Man" Randy Savage & Sting by disqualification

October 13, 1996 Tupelo, Mississippi

"Macho Man" Randy Savage defeated The Giant & Sting by disqualification

October 18, 1996 Minneapolis, Minnesota

"Macho Man" Randy Savage defeated The Giant & Sting by disqualification

November 1, 1996 Hammond, Indiana

Sting defeated "Macho Man" Randy Savage & The Giant by count-out

November 2, 1996 Battle Creek, Michigan

Sting defeated "Macho Man" Randy Savage & The Giant by count-out

November 3, 1996 Saginaw, Michigan

Sting defeated "Macho Man" Randy Savage & The Giant by count-out

November 23, 1996 Baltimore, Maryland

The Giant defeats Sting by disqualification

November 30, 1996 Charleston, South Carolina

"Enforcer" Arn Anderson defeated Sting by count-out

December 2, 1996 Monday Nitro Dayton, Ohio

Rick Steiner defeats Sting by count-out

December 16, 1996 Monday Nitro Pensacola, Florida

Rick Steiner vs Sting declared a no contest

January 3, 1997 Little Rock, Arkansas

Sting vs. The Giant ended in a no contest, this was a house show and would be his final match for almost a year.

The Final Matches of "Macho Man" Randy Savage

In the days leading up to WrestleKingdom 2020 I found myself with a few days off and I decided to check out some of the prior January 4th shows at the Tokyo Dome. I found some great matches and at times unexpected wrestlers on the shows. One of those was on January 4, 2000, the show was then called Wrestling World, and "Macho Man" Randy Savage wrestled Rick Steiner.

Two things immediately came to mind when I saw this; I don't think I've ever seen them wrestle before and I don't remember Macho Man wrestling in the year 2000, I thought he had left WCW by then. That was 20 years ago though, so why would I even remember this. Using my normal sources Cage Match and The History of WWE plus a few other places I was surprised by what I discovered about the Macho Man's finals days in the ring.

His last match in 1999 was on August 14th at the Road Wild PPV when he defeated Dennis Rodman in a hardcore match. On October 25th he appeared on Nitro in Phoenix, Arizona cutting a promo on Vince Russo and The New Blood, saying what they did to Hogan and Flair they could never do to him because he wasn't a punk bitch. He talked about being a world champion in WWE & WCW and that he was looking to pass the torch to someone. Savage was 47 years old at this point.

His next wrestling appearance came at that January 4th Tokyo Dome show for New Japan, his first appearance in New Japan since 1996. In this match with Rick Steiner Savage was filling in for an injured Goldberg.

His next match was also filling in for an injured Goldberg, this time against Sid Vicious at a WCW House show on January 14, 2000 in Charleston, West Virginia and was pinned by Sid after a powerbomb. This would end up being the final singles match of Savage's career.

His next WCW TV appearance was on the May 2, 2000 episode of Thunder from the historic Mid-South Coliseum in Memphis, Tennessee. During the main event number 1 contender Battle Royal Savage made a surprise appearance 20 minutes into the 23 minute match that Ric Flair would go on to win. This was also Randy's final WCW appearance.

We wouldn't see the Macho Man in a wrestling ring again until late 2004 in TNA. Well technically he did appear in a wrestling ring on the season 1 episode 14 of Nikki a wrestling themed situational comedy where he played James "Pretty Boy" Carter and as Bonesaw McGraw in 2002 for Sam Raimi's Spider-Man. He looked awesome in both.

On November 7, 2004 TNA presented Victory Road their first ever 3 hour monthly PPV. At the conclusion of the main event Savage made a surprise appearance confronting NWA World Champion Jeff Jarrett.

He appeared on the November 19th and 26th episodes of Impact confronting Jarrett, Scott Hall, & Kevin Nash building towards a six man tag team match at the next TNA PPV. At Turning Point on December 5th, Savage teamed with AJ Styles and Jeff Hardy defeating Jarrett, Nash, & Hall in a six man tag team match.

I wouldn't say Savage looked bad in the match but he wasn't the Savage of old. He'd lost a lot of muscle mass and even covered himself wearing a long sleeve shirt and loose pants. Earlier in the evening Savage was attacked in the back and stuffed in the trunk of a car that sped away after. With a three on two advantage Jarrett, Nash, & Hall got the best of Hardy and Styles for over 15 minutes before Savage walked to the ring.

Tagging himself in he went to work with punches on Jarrett, then Hall & Nash. There was a three way sleeper hold but Jarrett got out of his. Jarrett then attempted a sunset flip but Savage punched him in the face and then sat down on Jarrett's chest hooking the leg for the three count, pinning the NWA World Champion.

I've read that this was supposed to lead to Savage defeating Jarrett for the championship at the January Final Resolution PPV and losing it back to Jarrett at the February Against All Odd PPV. Imagine Randy Savage's name in the history books as a former NWA World Champion. He and Flair would then be the only ones to hold the WWE, NWA, & WCW World Championships.

Before anyone says but Kurt Angle the answer is no. Kurt Angle was the first ever TNA World Champion, yes he held up the NWA Championship up after defeating Sting and Christian Cage at Sacrifice 2007 however, the NWA had stripped Cage and Team 3D of their NWA Championships earlier that day. Also when Kurt Angle won the WCW Championship, it was in namesake only as World Championship Wrestling had ceased to exist.

It's odd to me that Savage didn't wrestle during that time between WCW & TNA. Perhaps he had one of those Time Warner contracts that prevented him. I always think it's sad when a wrestler, especially the one the caliber or Randy Savage, doesn't get the big sendoff that I feel they deserve. It's nice that he was inducted into the WWE Hall of Fame in 2015, but it would have been better if he could have been there himself to accept it.

Update

In 2012 Macho Man was featured in WWE All Stars video game and he even cut a couple promos for the video game and speculation was he was going to return to the promotion, but he passed away. You can find the promo on YouTube, it's pretty cool.

I saw Macho Man live twice, the first time was on June 4, 1989 at the Cumberland County Civic Center in Portland, Maine for a WWE house show. This was my first ever live wrestling event. Savage with Sensational Sherri defeated WWE World Champion: Hulk Hogan by count-out.

The second time was on June 9, 1997 in Boston, Massachusetts at WCW Monday Nitro, we had second row seats! He didn't wrestle that night however he did cut a promo that night where Diamond Dallas Page ran in and they fought inside and all along the outside of the ring, it was excellent!

Authors Note

The next several chapters I take a deep dive into statistics of wrestling championships both active and inactive. The promotions I examine in these chapters are the major North American ones. When it comes to the NWA some of their championships will be grouped with the WCW title lineages and I will not be looking at all the regional championships. The United States Championship lineage starts with the NWA, then WCW, and currently with the WWE.

The lineage used for the current NWA championships are as follows. The NWA World title has unbroken lineage going back to 1948. This version of the World Television Championship goes back to January 2020. The National Championship can be traced back to 1980. The World Tag Team championships were first crowned in WCW in 1992. The NWA Women's Championship is the most confusing. NWA recognized Mildred Burk from 1950 – 1953, this championship she first won in 1935. Then the lineage is disputed as The Fabulous Moolah was recognized in the Northeast from 1956 – 1983 whereas June Byers was recognized in the rest of the NWA from 1954 until 1964. From 1986 – 1996 sporadically the title is recognized. The title was brought back in the year 2002 with consistent champions and minimal vacancies until today where Thunder Rosa is the current champion as of publication. For my title history chapters I will be referring the lineage of the championship from August 23, 2002 to today.

Active Championships

WWE
WWE World Champion
Universal Champion
Intercontinental Champion
United States Champion
Raw Tag Team Champions

Smackdown Tag Team Champions
Raw Women's Champion
Smackdown Women's Champion
Women's Tag Team Champions
24/7 Champion

NXT
NXT Champion
Women's Champion
North American Champion
Tag Team Champions
Cruiserweight Champion

NXT-UK
NXT United Kingdom Champion
Women's Champion
Tag Team Champions

NWA
World Heavyweight Champion
World Television Champion
National Heavyweight Champion
World Tag Team Champions
Women's Champion

AEW
World Heavyweight Champion
World Women's Champion
World Tag Team Champion
TNT Champion

TNA / Impact
World Heavyweight Champion
X-Division Champion
World Tag Team Champions
Knockout's Champion

ROH
World Heavyweight Champion
World Television Champion
World Tag Team Champions
World Six-Man Tag Team Champions

Inactive Championships

WWE
World Heavyweight Champion 09/2/2002 – 12/15/2013
Hardcore Champion 11/2/1998 – 08/26/2002
European Champion 02/26/1997 – 7/22/2002
Light-Heavyweight Champion 12/07/1997 – 11/30/2001
Cruiserweight Champion (WCW) 03/20/1996 – 09/28/2007
World Tag Team Champions 06/03/1971 – 08/16/2010
Women's Champion 09/18/1956 – 09/19/2020
Divas Champion 07/20/2008 – 04/03/2016
Women's Tag Team Champions 05/13/1983 – 07/14/1989

WW-ECW Champion 06/13/2006 – 02/16/2010

ECW
World Heavyweight Champion 04/25/1992 – 04/04/2001
World Television Champion 08/12/1992 – 04/04/2001
World Tag Team Champion 06/23/1992 - 04/04/2001

NWA/WCW
WCW World Heavyweight Champion 01/11/1991 – 12/09/2001
World Television Champion 02/27/1974 – 04/10/2000
International World Heavyweight Champion 09/1993 – 06/23/1994
World Tag Team Champions 01/29/1975 – 11/28/2001
United States Tag Team Champions 09/28/1986 – 07/31/1992
World Six-Man Tag Team Champions 02/17/1991 – 11/1991
Hardcore Champion 07/11/1999 – 03/26/2001
Light Heavyweight Champion 10/27/1991 – 09/02/1992

Cruiserweight Tag Team Champions 03/18/2001 – 03/26/2001
Women's Champion 12/29/1996 - late 1997
Women's Cruiserweight Champion 04/07/1997 - late 1997

TNA / Impact
Knockouts Tag Team Champions 9/20/2009 – 06/20/2013
Grand Champion 10/02/2016 – 06/04/2018
Legends/Global/Television/King of the Mountain Champion
10/23/2018 – 08/13/2016

ROH Pure Champion 02/12/2004 – 08/12/2006
WOH World Women's Champion 12/15/2017 - 01/01/2020

Longest Reigning Champions

First published on August 14, 2016, it has been updated as needed

In this chapter we will take a look at the longest single continuous reign of each of the major championships past and present from promotions based in the United States.

Active Championships

WWE World Heavyweight Championship
Bruno Sammartino
May 17, 1963 - January 18, 1971 2,803 days
Bruno defeated Buddy Rogers and was defeated by Ivan Koloff both matches took place at Madison Square Garden in New York

WWE Universal Championship
Brock Lesnar
April 2, 2017 – August 19, 2018 504 days
Lesnar defeated Goldberg at WrestleMania 33 in Orlando, Florida and was defeated by Roman Reigns at SummerSlam in Brooklyn, New York

WWE Intercontinental Championship
The Honky Tonk Man
June 2, 1987 - August 29, 1988 454 days

Honky defeated Ricky "The Dragon" Steamboat in Buffalo, New
York and was defeated by The Ultimate Warrior at SummerSlam
at Madison Square Garden

WWE / WCW United States Championship
"Total Package" Lex Luger
May 22, 1989 - October 27, 1990 523 days
Luger defeated Michael "P.S." Hayes in Bluefield, West Virginia
and was defeated by Stan "The Lariat" Hansen at Halloween
Havoc in Chicago, Illinois

WWE Raw Tag Team Championship
The New Day: Big E, Kofi Kingston, & Xavier Woods
August 23, 2015 - December 18, 2016 483 days
They defeated The Prime Time Players: Darren Young & Titus
O'Neil at SummerSlam in Brooklyn, New York and were defeated
by Cesaro & Sheamus at Roadblock: End of the Line in Pittsburgh,
Pennsylvania.

WWE SmackDown Tag Team Championships
The Usos: Jimmy & Jey
October 8, 2017 - April 8, 2018 182 days
They defeated The New Day: Big E, Kofi Kingston, & Xavier
Woods at Hell in a Cell in Detroit, Michigan and were defeated by
The Bludgeon Brothers: Harper & Rowan at WrestleMania 34 in
New Orleans, Louisiana

WWE Raw Women's Championship
Becky Lynch
April 8, 2019 - May 11, 2020 399 days
Lynch defeated Ronda Rousey & Charlotte Flair at WrestleMania
35 in East Rutherford, New Jersey and surrendered the
championship to Asuka on May 11, 2020 on a taped Monday Night
Raw revealing that she was pregnant. This was actually taped on
April 15, 2020 but aired on the USA network on May 11th. WWE
officially recognizes her reign as being 398 days ending at Money

in the Bank PPV.

WWE SmackDown Women's Championship
Bayley
October 11, 2019 to current
Bayley defeated Charlotte Flair at SmackDown in Paradise, Nevada and as of publication is the current champion

WWE Women's Tag Team Championships
The Kabuki Warriors: Asuka & Kairi Sane
October 6, 2019 - April 4, 2020 180 days
The Warrior's defeated Nikki Cross & Alexa Bliss at Hell in a Cell in Sacramento, California and were defeated by Nikki Cross & Alexa Bliss at WrestleMania 36 in Orlando, Florida. Again the date of this reign could be debated as the match was pretaped, however the match aired on April 4th.

NXT Championship
Adam Cole
June 1, 2019 – July 8, 2020 403 days
Cole defeated Johnny Gargano at TakeOver XXV in Bridgeport, Connecticut and was defeated by Keith Lee in Winter Park, Florida

NXT North American Championship
Velveteen Dream
February 20, 2019 - September 18, 2019 209 days
Dream defeated Johnny Gargano and was defeated by Roderick Strong, both matches happened at Full Sail University in Winter Park, Florida. The length of this reign is also disputed as the match where Dream won was taped on January 30, 2019. However, two finishes were taped with Dream winning and Gargano winning, it wasn't revealed who officially won the championship until the match aired.

NXT Tag Team Championships
The Ascension: Konnor & Viktor
September 12, 2013 - September 11, 2014 364 days
They defeated Adrian Neville & Corey Graves and were defeated
by The Lucha Dragons: Kalisto & Sin Cara both matches were at
Full Sail University in Winter Park, Florida

NXT Cruiserweight Championship
Neville now known as Pac
January 29, 2017 - August 14, 2017 197 days
He defeated Rich Swann at the Royal Rumble in San Antonio,
Texas and was defeated by Akira Tozawa in Boston,
Massachusetts

NXT Women's Championship
Asuka
April 1, 2016 - September 6, 2017 522 days
She defeated Bayley at TakeOver Dallas in Texas and vacated the
championship when she moved to the main roster. It should be
noted that she broke her collarbone on August 19th at TakeOver
Brooklyn III, the segment when she surrendered the championship
was taped on August 24th and aired September 6th.

NXT United Kingdom Championship
"Bruiserweight" Pete Dunne
May 20, 2017 - April 5, 2019 685 days
Dunne defeated Tyler Bate at TakeOver Chicago in Illinois and
was defeated by Walter at NXT TakeOver New York in Brooklyn

NXT United Kingdom Tag Team Championships
Gallus: Wolfgang & Mark Coffey
October 4, 2019 - current
Gallus defeated Mark Andrews & Flash Morgan Webster in
Cardiff, Wales and as of publication are the current champions

NXT United Kingdom Women's Championship
Kay Lee Ray
August 31, 2019 - current
Ray defeated Toni Storm at NXT UK TakeOver Cardiff in Wales
and as of publication is the current champion

AEW World Heavyweight Championship
Chris Jericho
August 21, 2019 - February 29, 2020 182 days
Jericho defeated Hangman Page in a tournament final to become
the first champion at All Out in Hoffman Estates, Illinois and was
defeated by Jon Moxley at Revolution in Chicago

AEW TNT Championship
Cody Rhodes
May 23, 2020 - current
Cody defeated Lance Archer in a tournament final at Double or
Nothing in Jacksonville, Florida to become the first champion and
as of publication is the current champion

AEW World Tag Team Championship
Kenny Omega & "Hangman" Adam Page
January 21, 2020 - current
They defeated SCU: Frankie Kazarian & Scorpio Sky in Nassau,
Bahamas and and as of publication are the current champions

AEW World Women's Championship
Riho
October 2, 2019 - February 12, 2020 133 days
Riho defeated Nylas Rose on the debut episode of Dynamite to
become the first champion in Washington D.C. and she was
defeated by Nyla Rose in Cedar Park, Texas

NWA World Heavyweight Championship
Lou Thesz
November 27, 1949 - March 15, 1956 1,941 Days

Thesz was awarded the championship after then champion Orville Brown suffered career ending injuries in an automobile accident on November 1, 1949. He was defeated by Whipper Billy Watson in Toronto, Ontario, Canada

NWA World Television Championship
Zicky Dice
January 26, 2020 – current
Dice defeated Ricky Starks in Atlanta, Georgia and as of publication is the current champion

NWA National Heavyweight Championship
Phil Shatter
January 17, 2009 – February 19, 2011 763 days
Defeated Crusher Hansen in McKeesport, Pennsylvania and was defeated by Chance Prophet in Franklinville, New Jersey

NWA World Tag Team Championships
The Skullkrushers: Keith Walker & Rasche Brown
October 4, 2008 – November 20, 2010 777 days
They defeated Los Luchas: Phoenix Star & Zokre in Robstown, Texas and were defeated by The Dark City Fight Club: Jon Davis & Kory Chavis in Milwaukee, Wisconsin

NWA World Women's Championship
Jazz
September 16, 2016 – April 22, 2019 948 days
Defeated Amber Gallows in Sherman, Texas and vacated the championship for medical and personal reasons

TNA/ Impact World Heavyweight Champion
Bobby Roode
October 26, 2011 - July 8, 2012 256 days
Roode defeated James Storm in Macon, Georgia and was defeated by Austin Aries at Desination X Pay-Per-View in Orlando, Florida

TNA / Impact X-Division Championship
Austin Aries
September 11, 2011 - July 8, 2012 301 days
Aries defeated Brian Kendrick at the No Surrender Pay-Per-View
in Orlando, Florida and vacated for TNA / Impact World
Championship title match

TNA / Impact World Tag Team Championships
The North: "Walking Weapon" Josh Alexander & "All Ego" Ethan
Page
July 5, 2019 - current
The North defeated LAX: Latin American Exchange: Santana &
Ortiz at Bash at the Brewery in San Antonio, Texas and as of
publication are the current champions

TNA / Impact Knockouts Championship
Taya Valkyrie
January 6, 2019 - January 18, 2020 377 days
Taya defeated Tessa Blachard at Homecoming in Nashville,
Tennessee and was defeated by Jordynne Grace in Mexico City,
Mexico

ROH World Heavyweight Championship
Samoa Joe
March 22, 2003 - December 26, 2004 645 days
Joe defeated Xavier was defeated by Austin Aries both matches
took place in Philadelphia, Pennsylvania

ROH World Television Championship
Jay Lethal
April 4, 2014 - October 23, 2015 567 days
Lethal defeated Tommaso Ciampa in New York City was defeated
by Roderick Strong in Kalamazoo, Michigan

ROH World Tag Team Championship
The Kings of Wrestling: Chris Hero & Claudio Castagnoli
April 3, 2010 - April 1, 2011 363 days
The Kings defeated The Briscoe Brothers: Mark & Jay in
Charlotte, North Carolina were defeated by Wrestling Greatest Tag
Team: Charlie Haas & Shelton Benjamin in Toronto, Ontario,
Canada

ROH World Six-Man Tag Team Championship
Villain Enterprises: Marty Scurll, Brody King, & PCO
March 16, 2019 - January 11, 2020 301 days
They defeated The Kingdom: Matt Taven, TK O'Ryan, & Vinny
Marseglia in Sunrise Manor, Nevada and were defeated by Mexa
Squad: Bandido, Flamita, & Rey Horus in Atlanta, Georgia

Inactive Championships

WWE World Championship
Batista
April 3, 2005 - January 10, 2006 282 days
Batista defeated Triple H at WrestleMania 21 in Los Angeles,
California and he vacated the championship due to injury

WWE Hardcore
Big Boss Man
October 12, 1999 - January 17, 2000 97 days
Boss Man defeated Al Snow in Albany, New York and was
defeated by Test in New Haven, Connecticut

WWE European Championship
"British Bulldog" Davey Boy Smith
February 26, 1997 - September 20, 1997 206 days
Smith defeated Owen Hart in a tournament final in Berlin,
Germany and was defeated by "Heartbreak Kid" Shawn Michaels
at One Night Only in Birmingham, England

WWE Light Heavyweight Championship
Duane Gill/Gillberg
November 17, 1998 - February 13, 2000 453 days
Gill defeated Christian in Columbus, Ohio was defeated by Essa
Rios w/ Lita in Austin, Texas

WWE / WCW Cruiserweight Championship
Gregory Helms
January 29, 2006 - February 18, 2007 385 days
Helms defeated Kid Kash at the Royal Rumble in Miami, Florida
and was defeated by Chavo Guerrero at No Way Out in Los
Angeles, California

WWE World Tag Team Championships
Demolition: Ax & Smash
March 27, 1988 - July 18, 1989 478 days
They defeated Strike Force: Rick Martel & Tito Santana at
WrestleMania IV in Atlantic City, New Jersey and lost them to
The Brain Busters: "Enforcer" Arn Anderson & Tully Blanchard at
Saturday Night's Main Event in Worcester, Massachusetts

WWE Women's Championship
The Fabulous Moolah
September 18, 1956 - June 23, 1984 10,170 days
Moolah last eliminated Judy Grable in 13 Woman battle royal in
Baltimore, Maryland and was defeated by Wendi Richter at the
Brawl to End it All at Madison Square Garden

WWE Divas Championship
Nikki Bella
November 23, 2014 - September 20, 2015 301 days
Nikki defeated AJ Lee at the Survivor Series in St. Louis, Missouri
and was defeated by Charlotte Flair at Night of Champions in
Houston, Texas

WWE Women's Tag Team Championship
The Glamour Girls: Judy Martin & Leilani Kai
August 1985 - January 24, 1988 906 days
They defeated Velvet McIntyre & Princess Victoria in Pittsburgh,
Pennsylvania and were defeated by The Jumping Bomb Angels:
Noriyo Tateno & Itsuki Yamazaki at the first Royal Rumble in
Hamilton, Ontario, Canada

WW-ECW Championship
Christian
July 26, 2009 - February 16, 2010 205 days
defeated "The Innovator of Violence" Tommy Dreamer at Night of
Champions in Philadelphia, Pennsylvania and was defeated by
Ezekiel Jackson in Kansas City, Missouri

ECW World Heavyweight
"Franchise" Shane Douglas
November 30, 1997 - January 10, 1999 406 days
defeated Bam Bam Bigelow at November to Remember in
Monaca, Pennsylvania and was defeated by Taz at Guilty As
Charged in Kissimmee, Florida

ECW World Television
Rob Van Dam
April 4, 1998 - March 4, 2000 700 days
RVD defeated Bam Bam Bigelow in Buffalo, New York and
vacated the championship due to an injury

ECW World Tag Team Championship
The Super Destroyers: AJ Petrucci & Doug Stahl
June 23, 1992 - April 2, 1993 283 days
They won a tournament final defeating Glen Osbourne & Max
Thrasher in Philadelphia, Pennsylvania and were defeated by Tony
Stetson & Larry Winters in Radnor, Pennsylvania

WCW World Heavyweight Championship
"Immortal" Hulk Hogan
July 17, 1994 - October 29, 1995 469 days
Hogan defeated "Nature Boy" Ric Flair at Bash of the Beach Pay-Per-View in Orlando, Florida and was defeated by The Giant at Halloween Havoc Pay-Per-View in Detroit, Michigan
NWA/WCW World Television
Tully Blanchard
March 28, 1984 - March 16, 1985 353 days a
Blanchard defeated Mark Youngblood in Spartanburg, South Carolina and was defeated by "The American Dream" Dusty Rhodes in Greensboro, North Carolina

WCW International World Heavyweight Championship
"Ravishing" Rick Rude
September 19, 1993 - March 16, 1994 178 days
Rude defeated "Nature Boy" Ric Flair at Fall Brawl 1993 Pay-Per-View and lost to Hiroshi Hase in Tokyo, Japan

WCW World Tag Team
Doom: Ron Simmons & "Hacksaw" Butch Reed
May 19, 1990 - February 24, 1991 281 days
Doom defeated The Steiner Brothers: Rick & Scott at Capital Combat Pay-Per-View in Washington DC and were defeated by The Fabulous Freebirds: Michael P.S. Hayes & Jimmy Garvin at Wrestle War Pay-Per-View in Phoenix, Arizona

NWA / WCW United States Tag Team Championship
Midnight Express: "Beautiful" Bobby Eaton & "Sweet" Stan Lane
May 16, 1987 - April 26, 1988 345 days
The Midnights won tournament defeating Barry Windham & "Rugged" Ronnie Garvin in Atlanta, Georgia and were defeated by The Fantastics: Bobby Fulton & Tommy Rogers in Chattanooga, Tennessee

WCW World Six-Man Tag Team Championship
Junkyard Dog, Ricky Morton, & "Wildfire" Tommy Rich
February 17, 1991 - June 3, 1991 106 days
Won a tournament final defeating "Nature Boy" Buddy Landel,
Dutch Mantel, & Dr. X in Atlanta, Georgia and was defeated by
The Fabulous Freebirds: Michael P.S. Hayes, Jimmy Garvin, &
Badstreet (Brad Armstrong) in Birmingham, Alabama

WCW Hardcore Championship
Norman Smiley
November 21, 1999 - January 12, 2000 51 days
Smiley won tournament defeating "Nasty Boy" Brian Knobs at the
Mayhem Pay-Per-View in Toronto, Ontario, Canada and was
defeated by "Nasty Boy" Brian Knobs in Erie, Pennsylvania

WCW Cruiserweight Tag Team
Kid Romeo & Elix Skipper
March 18, 2001 - March 26, 2001 8 days
Romeo & Skipper won a tournament defeating Billy Kidman &
Rey Mysterio Jr. at Greed Pay-Per-View in Jacksonville, Florida
and was defeated by Billy Kidman & Rey Mysterio Jr. at the final
WCW Monday Nitro in Panama City Beach, Florida

WCW Women's Championship
Akira Hokuto
December 29, 1996 - June 15, 1997 168 days
Hokuto won a tournament final defeating Madusa at Starrcade in
Nashville, Tennessee and the title vacated. It was later recognized
in GAEA until April 2018

WCW Women's Cruiserweight
Toshie Uematsu
April 7, 1997 - July 19, 1997 103 days
Toshie won a tournament final defeating Malia Hosaka in
Huntsville, Alabama and was defeated by Yoshiko Tamura in
Yokohama, Japan. The title was recognized in GAEA until April

2018

TNA Knockouts Tag Team Championship
ODB & Eric Young
February 28, 2012 - June 20, 2013 478 days
They defeated Gail Kim & Madison Rayne in Orlando, Florida and
the titles were vacate because Eric Young wasn't a women, yes it
took 478 days to decide this

TNA King of the Mountain Championship (formerly known as Legends, Global, & Television Championships)
Abyss
June 2, 2013 - July 3, 2014 396 days
Abyss defeated Devon at SlammiversaryXI in Boston,
Massachusetts the title was vacated because no defenses for 10
months

ROH Pure Championship
Nigel McGuinness
August 27, 2005 - August 12, 2006 350 days
Nigel defeated Samoa Joe in Buffalo, New York and was defeated
by Bryan Danielson in Liverpool, England when the title was
unified with the ROH World Championship

Women of Honor World Championship
Sumie Sakai
April 7, 2018 - December 14, 2018 251 days
Sakai was the first champion defeating Kelly Klein in a tournament
final in New Orleans, Louisiana and was defeated by Kelly Klein
at Final Battle in New York City

One Day Champions

First published on July 3, 2016 updated as appropriate

This year at WrestleMania XXXII in Dallas, Texas Zack Ryder won the 7 Man Ladder Match to become the Intercontinental Champion. The next night he lost it on Raw to The Miz, making him a one day champion. However, I don't think the length of his Championship reign diminishes the fact that he won the title in a hard fought contest and he can always claim that he is a former Intercontinental Champion.

So that got me thinking how many other one day champions have there been? Continue reading and you'll find the answer. I'm going to list the match in which they won the championship and then explain how they lost it. I'm going to start with active championships and then inactive ones. Also, I am only going to list officially recognized title changes.

The Hardcore Championship is not going to be listed, but for those wondering there were 169 title reigns that last one day or less. Incidentally Shawn Stasiak is a fifteen time Hardcore Champion whose combined reigns is less than one day. I am not including the WWE 24/7 Championship for the same reason, there have been 63 one day or less reigns of that Championship.

I did not include TNA Championships because too many of them were recorded on the same evening for tape delayed airing weeks or months later. All Elite Wrestling, NXT, & NXTUK has had no one day champions.

Active Championships

WWE World Heavyweight Championship

February 5, 1998 Indianapolis, Indiana The Main Event
Andre The Giant pinned Hulk Hogan
This was the famous twin referee angle where the evil Hebner
counted Hogan out even though his shoulder was clearly off the
mat. After winning the title Andre surrendered it to the "Million
Dollar Man" Ted Dibiase ending his title reign at under 10
minutes.

December 3, 1991 San Antonio, Texas This Tuesday in Texas
Hulk Hogan pinned The Undertaker
This match took place six days after their match at the Survivor
Series which saw Undertaker defeat Hogan for the title in
controversial fashion. President Jack Tunney was sitting ringside
for the rematch and witnessed Hogan use ashes from the
Undertaker's urn to win the bout. Hogan was stripped of the title
the next day, earning him a one day reign.

April 4, 1993 Las Vegas, Nevada WrestleMania IX
Yokozuna pinned Bret "Hitman" Hart after Mr. Fuji threw salt in
Hart's eyes
Hulk Hogan came out to check on Hart and Fuji immediately
challenged Hogan on behalf of Yokozuna. With Hart's blessing
Hogan accepted the challenge and 22 seconds after the bell was
rung and some miss-thrown salt Hogan pinned Yokozuna for his
5th title win.

February 16, 1997 Chattanooga, Tennessee In Your House 13:
Final Four
Bret "Hitman" Hart defeated "Stone Cold" Steve Austin, The
Undertaker, & Vader in a four way over the top rope elimination

match
The next night on Raw Hart was defending the championship
against Sid when Austin interfered, hitting Hart with a steel chair,
costing him the match and ending his title reign at one day.

June 28, 1998 Pittsburgh, Pennsylvania King of the Ring
Kane defeated "Stone Cold" Steve Austin in a first blood match
The next night on Raw Austin goaded Kane into a rematch,
reclaiming the championship and to date Kane's only reign with
the championship.

August 22, 1999 Minneapolis, Minnesota SummerSlam
Mankind defeated Steve Austin & Triple H in a triple threat match
The next night on Raw Triple H defeated Mankind with special
guest referee Shane McMahon. This match signified Mankind's
last and Triple H's first championship reign.

October 7, 2007 Rosemont, Illinois No Mercy
Randy Orton was awarded the vacant championship
Triple H pinned Randy Orton
Randy Orton defeated Triple H in a Last Man Standing match
So this one is a bit confusing. John Cena had been the champion
for over a year when he tore his pectoral muscle. At the beginning
of the PPV Mr. McMahon awarded Randy Orton the championship
but then ordered him to defend it in the opening contest against
Triple H who defeated Orton for the belt. Three matches later,
Triple H then successfully defended that Championship against
Umaga. Later that night Triple H was forced to defend the title
against Randy Orton in a Last Man Standing match which Orton
won ending Triple H's sixth reign as champion with Orton
becoming a two time champion in the same event.

February 21, 2010 St. Louis, Missouri Elimination Chamber
John Cena defeated Sheamus, Triple H, Randy Orton, Ted
DiBiase, & Kofi Kingston to win the championship
Moments after winning Vince McMahon ordered John Cena to

defend the title against Batista who ended Cena's reign with an official time of the fall being 32 seconds.

July 25, 2011 Hampton, Virginia Raw
Rey Mysterio Jr. defeated The Miz in a tournament final for the vacant championship
John Cena pinned Rey Mysterio Jr.
CM Punk had defeated John Cena at Money in the Bank for the title the same night his contract expired. A tournament was held over two episodes of Raw with Mysterio winning the championship. Mysterio then accepted the challenge of John Cena and lost the title that same night to Cena.

August 18, 2013 Los Angeles, California SummerSlam
Daniel Bryan pinned John Cena
Moments after winning the title, Randy Orton cashed in his Money in the Bank and defeated Bryan after referee Triple H pedigreed him.

September 15, 2013 Detroit, Michigan Night of Champions
Daniel Bryan pinned Randy Orton
The next night on Raw Triple H stripped Bryan of the championship stating that referee Scott Armstrong had made a fast three count and Bryan was in on it. Daniel Bryan is the only person to have two single day or less WWE World Heavyweight Championship reigns.

November 22, 2015 Atlanta, Georgia Survivor Series
Roman Reigns defeated Dean Ambrose in a tournament final for the vacant championship
Seconds after winning, Sheamus brogue kicked Reigns then cashed in his Money in the Bank contract winning the title.

June 19, 2016 Paradise, Nevada Money in the Bank
Seth Rollins defeated Roman Reigns with the pedigree
Dean Ambrose pinned Seth Rollins

Moments after winning Dean Ambrose cashed in his Money in the Bank that he won that night to defeat Rollins.

WWE Universal Championship

August 21, 2016 Brooklyn, New York SummerSlam
Finn Balor defeated Seath Rollins
Finn became the first ever champion defeating Rollins in a tournament final, however he was injured during the match and had to surrender the championship the next night on Raw. As of this publication he has yet to recapture the championship.

WWE Intercontinental Championship

October 22, 1995 Winnipeg, Manitoba In Your House 4: Great White North
Dean Douglas was awarded the vacant championship
Razor Ramon pinned Dean Douglas
Shawn Michaels had been attacked outside a nightclub in Syracuse, NY the week prior. Douglas defended the championship that night, losing it to Razor Ramon.

July 24, 1999 Toronto, Ontario house show
Edge defeated Jeff Jarrett
The next night at Fully Loaded in Buffalo, NY Jarrett defeated Edge in a rematch

October 27, 2003 Fayetteville, North Carolina Raw
Chris Jericho defeated Rob Van Dam
Later that night in a steel cage match Van Dam regained the title from Jericho marking this as his shortest of his nine total reigns.

April 7, 2013 East Rutherford, New Jersey WrestleMania XXIX pre-show
The Miz defeated Wade Barrett
The next night at Raw Barrett regained the championship in a

rematch.

September 21, 2014 Nashville, Tennessee Night of Champions
The Miz defeated Dolph Ziggler
The next night at Raw Ziggler regained the championship in a
rematch.

April 3, 2016 Arlington, Texas WrestleMania XXXII
Zack Ryder won a 7 man ladder match defeating Dolph Ziggler,
Sami Zayn, Stardust, Kevin Owens, Sin Cara & The Miz
The next night on Raw The Miz defeated Ryder to win his fifth
championship.

NWA/WCW/WWE United States Championship

September 18, 1994 Roanoke, Virgina Fall Brawl 1994: War
Games
"Stunning" Steve Austin was awarded the title as Ricky "The
Dragon" Steamboat was unable to compete due to injury
Austin was forced to defend the title against "Hacksaw" Jim
Duggan who won the title in 35 seconds

April 19, 1998 Denver, Colorado Spring Stampede
Raven defeated Diamond Dallas Page in a Raven's Rules Match
The next night on WCW Monday Nitro Goldberg defeated Raven
extending his winning streak and winning his first ever
championship

August 10, 1998 Rapid City, South Dakota Monday Nitro
Lex Luger defeated Bret "Hitman" Hart
The next night at WCW Thunder in Fargo, ND Hart regained the
title in a re-match

October 24, 1999 Las Vegas, Nevada Halloween Havoc
Goldberg defeated Sid Vicious by referee stoppage\
The next night at Monday Nitro Bret Hart defeated Goldberg after

interference from the nWo

December 19, 1999 Washington DC Starrcade
Chris Benoit was awarded vacant title
Scott Hall has suffered a knee injury. At Starrcade, Benoit
defended the title against Jeff Jarrett in a ladder match. The next
night Nitro Jarrett defeated Benoit in a return ladder match.

September 22, 2000 Amarillo, Texas house show
Terry Funk defeated Lance Storm
The next night Funk lost the title to Storm in a rematch at another
house show in Lubbock, TX.

January 11, 2016 New Orleans, Louisiana Raw
Kalisto defeated Alberto Del Rio
The next night at the SmackDown taping Del Roi defeated Kalisto
in a rematch.

WWE Raw Tag Team Championships

October 24, 2010 Minneapolis, Minnesota Bragging Rights
The Nexus: John Cena & David Otunga defeated Drew McIntyre
& Cody Rhodes
The next night on Raw Heath Slater & Justin Gabriel won the titles
when Wade Barrett ordered David Otunga to be pinned keeping
the titles in The Nexus

February 20, 2011 Oakland, California Elimination Chamber
The Corre: Heath Slater & Justin Gabriel defeated Santino Marella
& Vladimir Kozlov
The next night on Raw, The Corre lost the titles to John Cena &
The Miz, however won them back later that evening.

April 8, 2018 New Orleans, Louisiana WrestleMania XXXIV
Braun Strowman & Nicholas defeated Cesaro & Sheamus
Strowman "randomly" picked a 10 year old out of the crowd to be

his tag team partner, Nicholas even tagged in at one point. The next night they relinquished the championships. Nicholas is the son of WWE referee John Cone who was the official in the ring during the match.

WWE Smackdown Women's Championship

May 19, 2019 Hartford, Connecticut Money in the Bank
Charlotte Flair defeated Becky Lynch
After defeated Becky Lynch in a hard fought match Bayley cashed in the Money in the Bank contract that she had won that same evening to defeat Charlotte and win the championship

NWA World Heavyweight Championship

August 27, 1994 Philadelphia, Pennsylvania
Shane Douglas defeated 2 Cold Scorpio in a tournament final for the vacant championship
After winning the title Douglas cut his famous promo throwing down the championship declaring it dead and proclaiming himself the ECW World Heavyweight Champion.

NWA World Tag Team Championships

March 22, 2001 Athens, Georgia
David Flair & Dan Factor defeated Bad Attitude: David Young & Rick Michaels, they lost the championships back to Bad Attitude the next day in Toccoa, Georgia

December 28, 2001 DeLand, Florida
Glacier & Jason Sugarman defeated The Heavenly Bodies: Chris Nelson & Vito DeNucci and lost the titles back to the Bodies the next day Live Oak, Florida

December 9, 2016 Ripley, Tennessee
The Heatseekers: Elliott Russell & Sigmon defeated The Iron

Empire: Rob Conway & Matt Riviera and lost the titles back to
Iron Empire the next day in Dyersburg, Tennessee

ROH World Tag Team Championships

May 15, 2004 Lexington, Massachuettes Round Robin Challenge
III
The Prophecy: BJ Whitmer & Dan Maff defeated Second City
Saints: CM Punk & Colt Cabana
The Briscoe Brothers: Mark & Jay defeated The Prophecy: BJ
Whitmer & Dan Maff
Second City Saints: CM Punk & Colt Cabana defeated The Briscoe
Brothers: Mark & Jay
This a unique night where the Second City Saints walked in and
out of the building as champions, but due to the nature of the event
the titles changed hands twice along the way in individual matches.

Inactive Championships

WWE World Championship

June 7, 2009 New Orleans, Louisiana Extreme Rules
Jeff Hardy defeated Edge in a ladder match
Moments later CM Punk cashed in his Money in the Bank winning
his second World Championship

February 15, 2011 San Diego, California SmackDown 600th
Episode
Dolph Ziggler was awarded the vacant championship
Co-General Manager Vickie Guerrero had banned the spear and
stripped Edge of the championship for using it, awarding the title
to her boyfriend Ziggler. Co-General Manager Teddy Long
granted Edge a title match that night, who won the championship
for the 7th time.

December 18, 2011 Baltimore, Maryland TLC
Big Show defeated Mark Henry in a chairs match
Moments later Daniel Bryan cashed in his Money in the Bank
contract

WWE European Championship

August 22, 1999 Minneapolis, Minnesota SummerSlam
Jeff Jarrett defeated D'Lo Brown winning the Eurocontinental
Championship
The next night on Raw Jarrett awarded the title to Mark Henry for
helping him defeat D'Lo Brown at SummerSlam.

April 2,2000 Anaheim, California WrestleMania 2000
Chris Jericho defeated Kurt Angle and Chris Benoit in a two fall
triple threat match where the second fall was for the European
Championship. The first fall had been for the Intercontinental
Championship. Jericho pinned Benoit.
The next night on Raw Eddie Guerrero defeated Jericho for the
championship.

WCW / WWE Cruiserweight Championship

October 4, 1999 Kansas City, Missouri Monday Nitro
Psychosis was awarded the vacant championship
Lenny Lane had been the champion since 8/19/1999 but was
stripped of the title by Turner Broadcasting due to publicity
backlash over Lane's homosexual character gimmick. Psychosis
lost the title to Disco Inferno the same night.

March 30, 2000 Baltimore, Maryland house show
Billy Kidman defeated The Artist
The next night The Artist regained the title at a house show in
Pittsburgh, PA.

WWE World Tag Team Championships

August 9, 1980 New York, New York Showdown at Shea
Bob Backlund & Pedro Morales defeated the Wild Samoans: Afa
& Sika in a two out of three falls match, two falls to none.
The next day Backlund & Morales were stripped of the titles
because Backlund was the current WWE World Heavyweight
Champion and by-laws at that time prevented a wrestler from
holding more than one title at a time.

January 22, 1995 Tampa, Florida Royal Rumble
The 1-2-3 Kid & Bob Holly defeated Bam Bam Bigelow &
Tatanka in a tournament final for the vacant championships
The next night on Raw the Smoking Gunns won the titles

September 24, 1995 Saginaw, Michigan In Your House: Triple
Header
Two Dudes with Attitudes: Diesel & Shawn Michaels defeated
Yokozuna & British Bulldog (substituting for Owen Hart) when
Owen was pinned
Yes Owen was pinned even though he was not involved in the
match. That is why the next night on Raw the titles were returned
to Owen and Yokozuna who then lost them that night to The
Smoking Gunns.

March 29, 1998 Boston, Massachusetts WrestleMania XIV
Cactus Jack & Chainsaw Charlie defeated The New Age Outlaws:
Billy Gunn & Road Dogg in a dumpster match
The next night on Raw the Outlaws regained the titles in a Steel
Cage Match

September 20, 1999 Houston, Texas Raw
The Rock n' Sock Connection: The Rock & Mankind defeated Big
Show & The Undertaker
The next night at the Smackdown taping The New Age Outlaws on
the titles.

October 22, 2000 Albany, New York No Mercy
Los Conquistadores defeated The Hardy Boyz
Edge & Christian were dressed as Los Conquistadores, the next
night on Raw E & C challenged Los Conquistadores to a match,
which they lost as now the Hardy's were in the costumes so
technically Edge & Christian won and then lost the belts to the
Hardy Boyz.

December 18,2000 Greenville, South Carolina Raw
The Rock & Undertaker defeated Edge & Christian
The next night E & C regained the titles with Kurt Angle as the
special guest referee

March 19, 2001 Albany, New York Raw
Edge & Christian defeated The Hardy Boyz
Later that same evening the Dudley Boyz beat Edge & Christian
for the titles

January 19, 2003 Boston, Massachusetts Royal Rumble
The Dudley Boyz defeated William Regal & Lance Storm
The next night on Raw Regal and Storm regained the titles.

WWE Women's Championship

January 31, 2000 Pittsburgh, Pennsylvania Raw
Hervina defeated The Kat in a lumberjill snowbunny match
Hervina is Harvey Wippleman in drag. He was defeated the next
night at the SmackDown taping by Jacqueline

September 17, 2006 Toronto, Ontario Unforgiven
Trish Stratus defeated Lita
This was Trish Stratus' retirement match and the title was vacated

April 24, 2007 Paris, France live event
Mickie James defeated Melina and Victoria in a triple threat match

Melina was awarded an immediate rematch as Victoria was pinned and not Melina, who went on to recapture the championship.

WWE Diva's Championship

October 12, 2009 Indianapolis, Indiana Raw
Jillian Hall pinned Mickie James
Jillian was forced to immediately defend her newly won championship against Melina losing it to her.

ECW World Heavyweight Championship

April 25, 1992 Mount Tabor, Pennsylvania house show
Jimmy "Superfly" Snuka defeated Salvator Bellomo in a tournament final
Snuka was the first ever champion but lost it the next night to Johnny Hotbody in Philadelphia, PA

April 22, 2000 Philadelphia, Pennsylvania ECW Arena CyberSlam 2000
Tommy Dreamer defeated Taz
Moments later Justin Credible goaded Dreamer into defending the championship where he defeated the innovator of violence.

January 7, 2001 New York, New York Guilty As Charged
The Sandman defeated Steve Corino & Justin Credible in a TLC & Canes match
Moments later Rhino was awarded a title shot defeating Sandman becoming the final champion.

WCW World Heavyweight Championship

April 19, 1998 Denver, Colorado Spring Stampede
"Macho Man" Randy Savage defeated Sting
The next night on Nitro Savage lost the Championship to "Hollywood" Hulk Hogan in a no disqualification match

April 26, 1999 Fargo, North Dakota Nitro
Sting defeated Diamond Dallas Page
That night Diamond Dallas Page regained the championship in a
Fatal Four-Way no DQ match that also featured Sting, Kevin Nash,
& Goldberg

July 11, 1999 Ft. Lauderdale, Florida Bash at the Beach
Randy Savage & Sid Vicious defeated Kevin Nash & Sting to win
the championship
Kevin Nash was the champion and as he was pinned by Savage in
the match he lost the title to him. The next night on Nitro Savage
was defeated by "Hollywood" Hulk Hogan

January 16, 2000 Cincinnati, Ohio Souled Out
Chris Benoit defeated Sid Vicious for the vacant championship
The next night Benoit quit WCW vacating the championship.
Storyline was Sid's foot was under
the ropes when he tapped out.

April 24, 2000 Rochester, New York Nitro
Diamond Dallas Page defeated Jeff Jarrett in a steel cage match
The next day at the Thunder taping Page teamed with David
Arquette against Eric Bischoff and Jeff Jarrett when the title was
on the line. Arquette pinned Bischoff, winning the championship.

May 22, 2000 Grand Rapids, Michigan Nitro
Jeff Jarrett defeated Kevin Nash in a falls out anywhere match for
the vacant championship
The next day at the Thunder taping Nash defeated Jarrett and Scott
Steiner in a triple threat match

May 29, 2000 Salt Lake City, Utah Nitro
"Nature Boy" Ric Flair was awarded the title by Kevin Nash
Flair had one the title on May 15th the suffered what was thought
to be a severe medical condition so he was stripped of the title on

May 22nd. When it was discovered that Flair medical cleared the
have Nash give Flair the belt back. Later that same night on the
29th Jeff Jarrett defeated Flair.

WCW World Television Championship

February 17, 1996 Baltimore, Maryland live event
Lex Luger defeated Johnny B. Badd
The next day in Norfolk, VA Badd regained the title

April 30, May 1 - 3, 1998
Chris Benoit & Booker T traded the title back and forth
4/30 Benoit beat Booker Augusta, Georgia
5/1 Booker beat Benoit Greenville, South Carolina
5/2 Benoit beat Booker Charleston, South Carolina
5/3 Booker beat Benoit Savannah, Georgia
5/4 Fit Finlay defeated Booker T Indianapolis, Indiana Nitro

WCW World Tag Team Championship

September 17, 1995 Asheville, North Carolina Fall Brawl
Harlem Heat: Booker T & Stevie Ray defeated Dick Slater and
Bunkhouse Buck
The next night on Nitro The American Males: Marcus Bagwell &
Scotty Riggs upset Harlem Heat for the titles.

February 23, 1997 Daly City, California SuperBrawl VII
Lex Luger & The Giant defeated the Outsiders
This was at the height of the nWo,the next night on Nitro Eric
Bischoff returned the titles to the Outsiders as Lex Luger scored
the victory and was not medically cleared to wrestle.

October 24, 1999 Las Vegas, Nevada Halloween Havoc
Heat: Booker T & Stevie Ray defeated Konnan & Billy Kidman
and Brian Knobbs & Morrus in a triple threat match
The next night on Nitro Konnan & Billy Kidman regained the titles

February 12, 2000 Oberhausen, Germany house show
The Harris Brothers: Ron & Don defeated The Mamalukes: Johnny
The Bull & Big Vito
The next night in Leipzig, Germany the Mamalukes regained the
titles

August 13, 2000 Vancouver, British Columbia New Blood Rising
Dark Carnival: The Great Muta & Vampiro defeated KroniK:
Brian Adams & Bryan Clark
The next night on Nitro Rey Mysterio Jr. & Juventud Guerrera
won the belts.

WCW Hardcore Championship

May 22, 2000 Grand Rapids, Michigan Nitro
Shane Douglas defeated Terry Funk
The next night on Thunder Funk regained the Championship

June 5, 2000 Atlanta, Georgia Nitro
Eric Bischoff defeated Terry Funk
The next night on Thunder Bischoff awarded the title to Big Vito
& Johnny the Bull

August 14, 2000 Kelowna, British Columbia Nitro
Carl Ouellet was awarded the title by Lance Storm
That night Ouellet was defeated by Norman Smiley

This was way more of a daunting task that I thought it would be. It
took me several hours to research and record this information. If
the championship is not listed then there were no one day reigns.

One Year Champions

First published on August 30, 2016 updated as appropriate

In this chapter I'm taking a look at the major North American Championships where someone held the title for a year or more in a single reign, not a combined one. When I was a kid growing up in the 1980's long championship reigns had been commonplace and for 30 they really weren't, save RVD's near two year run as ECW World Television Champion. We are now starting to see it again, granted I don't think we'll ever see another Bruno Sammartino type reign, but they are not playing hot potato with the championships like they were. As of publication there have been no one year champions in AEW

Active Championships

WWE World Heavyweight Championship

Bruno Sammartino
May 17, 1963 - January 18, 1971 2,803 days
Bruno defeated "Nature Boy" Buddy Rogers was defeated by "Russian Bear" Ivan Koloff both matches took place at Madison Square Garden

December 10, 1973 - April 30, 1977 1,237 days
Bruno defeated Stan "The Man" Stasiak at Madison Square Garden
and was defeated by "Superstar" Billy Graham in Baltimore
Maryland

Pedro Morales
February 8, 1971 - December 1, 1973 1,027 days
Pedro defeated "Russian" Ivan Koloff at Madison Square Garden
and was defeated by Stan 'The Man" Stasiak in Philadelphia,
Pennsylvania

Bob Backlund
February 20, 1978 - December 26, 1983 2,135 days
Backlund defeated "Superstar" Billy Graham was defeated by The
Iron Sheik both matches took place at Madison Square Garden

Hulk Hogan
January 23, 1984 - February 5, 1988 1,474 days
The Hulkster defeated The Iron Sheik at Madison Square Garden
and was defeated by Andre the Giant in Indianapolis, Indiana

"Macho Man" Randy Savage
March 27, 1988 - April 2, 1989 371 days
Savage defeated "Million Dollar Man" Ted Dibiase was defeated
by Hulk Hogan both matches were at a WrestleMania in Atlantic
City, New Jersey

John Cena
September 17, 2006 - October 2, 2007 380 Days
Cena defeated Edge at Unforgiven in Toronto, Ontario, Canada
and was forced to vacant due to injury, torn pectoral muscle

CM Punk
November 20, 2011 - January 27, 2013 434 Days
Punk defeated Alberto Del Rio at the Survivor Series in Madison
Square Garden and was defeated by The Rock at the Royal

Rumble in Phoenix, Arizona

AJ Styles
November 7, 2017 - November 13, 2018 371 days
Defeated Jinder Mahal in Manchester, England and was defeated
by Daniel Bryan in St. Louis, Missouri

WWE Universal Championship

Brock Lesnar
April 7, 2017 - August 19, 2018 504 days
Brock defeated Goldberg at WrestleMania XXXIII in Orlando,
Florida and was defeated by Roman Reigns at SummerSlam in
Brooklyn, New York

WWE Intercontinental Championship

Pedro Morales
November 23, 1981 - January 22, 1983 425 days
Morales defeated "Magnificent" Don Muraco lost the
championship back to "Magnificent" Don Muraco both matches
took place at Madison Square Garden

"Magnificent" Don Muraco
January 22, 1983 - February 11, 1984 385 days
Muraco defeated Pedro Morales at Madison Square Garden was
defeated by Tito Santana at the old Boston Garden in
Massachusetts

"Macho Man" Randy Savage
February 8, 1986 - March 29, 1987 414 days
Savage defeated Tito Santana at the old Boston Garden was
defeated by Ricky "The Dragon" Steamboat at WrestleMania III in
Pontiac, Michigan

The Honky Tonk Man
June 2, 1987 - August 29, 1988 454 days
Honky defeated Ricky "The Dragon" Steamboat in Buffalo, New
York was defeated by The Ultimate Warrior at SummerSlam in
East Rutherford, New Jersey

WWE / WCW United States Championship

"Total Package" Lex Luger
May 22, 1989 - October 27, 1990 523 days
Luger defeated Michael "PS" Hayes in Bluefield, West Virginia
and was defeated by Stan 'The Lariat" Hansen at Halloween Havoc
in Chicago, Illinois

"Ravishing" Rick Rude
November 19, 1991 - January 11, 1993 378 days
Rude defeated Sting at Clash of the Champions XVII in Savannah,
Georgia and was stripped due to a neck injury

WWE RAW Tag Team Championship

The New Day: Big E, Kofi Kingston, & Xavier Woods
August 23, 2015 - December 18, 2016 483 days
They defeated The Prime Time Players: Darren Young & Titus
O'Neil at SummerSlam in Brooklyn, New York and were defeated
by Cesaro & Sheamus at Roadblock: End of the Line in Pittsburgh,
Pennsylvania.

WWE Raw Women's Championship

Becky Lynch
April 8, 2019 - May 11, 2020 399 days
Lynch defeated Ronda Rousey & Charlotte Flair at WrestleMania
35 in East Rutherford, New Jersey and surrendered the
championship to Asuka on May 11, 2020 on a taped Monday Night
Raw revealing that she was pregnant. This was actually taped on
April 15, 2020 but aired on the USA network on May 11th. WWE
officially recognizes her reign as being 398 days ending at Money
in the Bank PPV.

NXT Champion

Adam Cole
June 1, 2019 – July 8, 2020 403 days
Cole defeated Johnny Gargano at TakeOver XXV in Bridgeport,
Connecticut and was defeated by Keith Lee in Winter Park, Florida

NXT Women's Championship

Asuka
April 1, 2016 - September 6, 2017 522 days
She defeated Bayley at TakeOver Dallas in Texas and vacated the
championship when she moved to the main roster. It should be
noted that she broke her collarbone on August 19th at TakeOver
Brooklyn III, the segment when she surrendered the championship

was taped on August 24th and aired September 6th.

Shayna Baszler
October 28, 2018 - December 18, 2019 416 days
She defeated at Kari Sane at WWE Evolution in Uniondale, New York and was defeated by Rhea Ripley in Winter Park, Florida

NXT United Kingdom Championship

"Bruiserweight" Pete Dunne
May 20, 2017 - April 5, 2019 685 days
Dunne defeated Tyler Bate at TakeOver Chicago in Illinois and was defeated by Walter at NXT TakeOver New York in Brooklyn

Walter
April 5, 2019 - current
Walter defeated "Bruiserweight" Pete Dunne at NXT TakeOver New York in Brooklyn and as of publication is the current champion

NWA National Heavyweight Championship

Doug Gilbert
October 24, 1998 – January 15, 2000 448 days
Gilbert defeated Stevie Richards in Cherry Hill, New Jersey at the NWA 50th Anniversary Show and was defeated by Don Brodie in Memphis, Tennessee

Hotstuff Hernandez
October 13, 2001 – January 11, 2003 455 days
Hernandez defeated Kevin Northcutt in St. Petersburg, Florida at the NWA 53rd Anniversary Show and was defeated by Ricky Murdock in Greenville, Mississippi

Ricky Murdock
January 11, 2003 – October 15, 2004 643 days

Murdock defeated Hotstuff Hernandez in Greenville, Mississippi
and was defeated by Spyder in Winnipeg, Manitoba, Canada at the
NWA 56th Anniversary Show

Phil Shatter
January 17, 2009 – February 19, 2011 763 days
Defeated Crusher Hansen in McKeesport, Pennsylvania and was
defeated by Chance Prophet in Franklinville, New Jersey

Chance Prophet
February 19, 2011 – March 29, 2012 404 days
Prophet defeated Phil Shatter in Franklinville, New Jersey and was
defeated by Kahagas in Miami, Florida

NWA World Tag Team Championship

The Skullkrushers: Keith Walker & Rasche Brown
October 4, 2008 – November 20, 2010 777 days
They defeated Los Luchas: Phoenix Star & Zokre in Robstown,
Texas and were defeated by The Dark City Fight Club: Jon Davis
& Kory Chavis in Milwaukee, Wisconsin

The Dark City Fight Club: Jon Davis & Kory Chavis
May 15, 2011 – December 15, 2012 580 days
Dark City defeated The Usual Suspects: Murder One & AJ Steele
in Warner Robins, Georgia and were defeated by The Kingz of
Underground: Ryan Genesis & Scot Summers

NWA World Women's Championship

Leilani Kai
March 12, 2003 – June 19, 2004 465 days
Kai defeated Madison in Nashville, Tennessee in a dark match at
an NWA TNA taping, was stripped of the championship for
missing title defenses

Christie Ricci
October 5, 2005 – January 27, 2007 476 days
Ricci defeated Lexie Fyfe in Nashville, Tennessee at the NWA 57th
Anniversary show and was defeated by MsChif in Lebanon,
Tennessee

MsChif
April 27, 2008 – July 24, 2010 818 days
MsChif defeated Amazing Kong in Cape Girardeau, Missouri and
was defeated by Tasha Simone in Lebanon, Tennessee

Tasha Simone
November 6, 2010 – November 6, 2011 365 days
Simone defeated Rachel to win the vacant championship and was
defeated by Tiffany Roxx in a no disqualification match both took
place in Lebanon, Tennessee

Kacee Carlisle
October 20, 2012 – January 25, 2014 462 days
Carlisle defeated Tasha Simone in Lebanon, Tennessee and was
defeated by Barbi Hayden in Cypress, Texas

Barbi Hayden
January 25, 2014 – February 7, 2015 378 days
Hayden defeated Kacee Carlisle in Cypress, Texas and was
defeated by Santana Garrett in Plant City, Florida

Jazz
September 16, 2016 – April 22, 2019 948 days
Defeated Amber Gallows in Sherman, Texas and vacated the
championship for medical and personal reasons

TNA / Impact World Tag Team Championships
The North: "Walking Weapon" Josh Alexander & "All Ego" Ethan
Page
July 5, 2019 - current

The North defeated LAX: Latin American Exchange: Santana &
Ortiz at Bash at the Brewery in San Antonio, Texas and as of
publication are the current champions

TNA / Impact Knockouts Championship
Taya Valkyrie
January 6, 2019 - January 18, 2020 377 days
Taya defeated Tessa Blachard at Homecoming in Nashville,
Tennessee and was defeated by Jordynne Grace in Mexico City,
Mexico

ROH World Heavyweight Championship

Samoa Joe
March 22, 2003 - December 26, 2004 645 days
Joe defeated Xavier was defeated by Austin Aries both matches
took place in Philadelphia, Pennsylvania

Bryan Danielson
September 17, 2005 - December 23, 2006 462 days
Dragon defeated James Gibson at Glory by Honor IV in Lake
Grove, New York and was defeated by Homicide at Final Battle in
New York City

Nigel McGuinness
October 6, 2007 - April 3, 2009 545 days
Nigel defeated Takeshi Morishima in Edison, New Jersey and was
defeated by Jerry Lynn at Supercard of Honor IV in Houston,
Texas

Jay Lethal
June 19, 2015 - August 19, 2016 427 days
Lethal defeated Jay Briscoe at Best in the World in New York City
and was defeated by Adam Cole at Death Before Dishonor XIV in
Las Vegas, Nevada

ROH World Television Championship

Jay Lethal
April 4, 2014 - October 23, 2015 567 days
Lethal defeated Tommaso Ciampa in New York City was defeated
by Roderick Strong in Kalamazoo, Michigan

Inactive Championships

WWE Light Heavyweight Championship

Duane Gill/Gillberg
November 17, 1998 - February 13, 2000 453 days
He defeated Christian in Columbus, Ohio and was defeated by
Essa Rios with Lita in Austin, Texas

WWE / WCW Cruiserweight Championship

Gregory Helms
January 29, 2006 - February 18, 2007 385 days
Helms defeated Kid Kash at the Royal Rumble in Miami, Florida
and was defeated by Chavo Guerrero at No Way Out in Los
Angeles, California

WWE World Tag Team Championships

The Valiant Brothers: Jimmy & Johnny
May 8, 1974 - May 13, 1975 370 days
They defeated Tony Garea & Dean Ho in Hamburg, Pennsylvania
and were defeated by Dominic DeNucci & Victor Rivera in
Philadelphia, Pennsylvania

Demolition: Ax & Smash
March 27, 1988 - July 18, 1989 478 days
They defeated Strike Force: Rick Martel & Tito Santana in
Syracuse, New York and were defeated by The Brain Busters:

"Enforcer" Arn Anderson & Tully Blanchard on Saturday Night's
Main Event in Worcester, Massachusetts

WWE Women's Championship

The Fabulous Moolah
September 18, 1956 - July 23, 1984 10,170 days
Moolah won a 13 women Battle Royal last eliminating Judy
Grable in Baltimore, Maryland and was defeated by Wendi Richter
at the Brawl to end it All at Madison Square Garden

July 9, 1986 - July 24, 1987 380 days
Moolah defeated Velvet McIntyre in Sydney, Australia was
defeated by Sensational Sherri in Houston, Texas

Sensational Sherri
July 24, 1987 - October 7, 1988 441 days
She defeated The Fabulous Moolah in Houston, Texas and was
was defeated by Rockin' Robin in Paris, France

Rockin' Robin
October 7, 1988 - February 21, 1990 502 days
She defeated Sensational Sherri in Houston, Texas and the title
was declared vacated due to inactivity

Trish Stratus
January 9, 2005 - April 2, 2006 448 days
Trish defeated Lita at New Years Revolution in San Juan, Puerto
Rico and was defeated by Mickie James at WrestleMania XXII in
Rosemont, Illinois

WWE Women's Tag Team Championship

Velvet McIntyre & Princess Victoria
May 13, 1983 - December 7, 1984 574 days

They defeated Judy Grable & Wendi Richter in Calgary, Alberta, Canada Princess Victoria suffered a career ending neck injury and Desiree Petersen was chosen to replace her champion. However, it is officially considered a separate title reign for Mcintyre lasting until August 1, 1985 making her champion for 811consecutive days.

The Glamour Girls: Judy Martin & Leilani Kai
August 1, 1985 - January 24, 1988 906 days
They defeated Velvet McIntyre & Desiree Petersen in Cairo, Egypt and were defeated by The Jumping Bomb Angels: Noriyo Tateno & Itsuki Yamazaki at the Royal Rumble in Hamilton, Ontario, Canada

WCW World Heavyweight Championship

Hulk Hogan
July 17, 1994 - October 29, 1995 469 days
Hogan defeated "Nature Boy" Ric Flair at Bash at the Beach in Orlando, Florida and was defeated by The Giant at Halloween Havoc in Detroit, Michigan

ECW World Heavyweight Championship

"Franchise" Shane Douglas
March 26, 1994 - April 15, 1995 385 days
He defeated Terry Funk in Devon, Pennsylvania and was defeated by The Sandman in Philadelphia, Pennsylvania

November 30, 1997 - January 10, 1999 406 days
Dougles defeated Bam Bam Bigelow at November to Remember in Monaca, Pennsylvania and was defeated by Taz Guilty as Charged in Kissimmee, Florida

ECW World Television Championship

Rob Van Dam
April 4, 1998 - March 4, 2000 700 days
RVD defeated Bam Bam Bigelow in Buffalo, New York and was
forced to vacate the championship due to injury

TNA Knockouts Tag Team Championship

ODB & Eric Young
February 28, 2012 - June 20, 2013 478 days
They defeated Gail Kim & Madison Rayne in Orlando, Florida and
the titles were vacated because Eric Young is male, deactivated
June 27, 2013

**TNA King of the Mountain Championship (formerly known as
Legends, Global, & Television Championships)**

Abyss
June 2, 2013 - July 3, 2014 396 days
Abyss defeated Devon at SlammiversaryXI in Boston,
Massachusetts the title was vacated because no defenses for 10
months

One Year Champions: NWA World Heavyweight Championship

First published on September 9, 2016 updated as appropriate

What you may have noticed is that the NWA World Heavyweight Championship was not included in the One Year Champions chapter. That is because the number of men that have accomplished this is so great that it deserves its own chapter.

Orville Brown
July 14, 1948 - November 1, 1949 476 days
Upon creation of the National Wrestling Alliance the current Midwest Wrestling Association World Champion was declared the first NWA World Heavyweight Champion. He had defeated Sonny Meyer in Des Moines, Iowa. He was stripped of the championship when he suffered a career ending car accident.

Lou Thesz
November 27, 1949 - March 15, 1956 2301 days
Thesz was the current National Wrestling Association World Champion having won the championship on July 20, 1948 from Wild Bill Longson in Indianapolis, Indiana. As he was scheduled

to face Orville Brown to unify the championships he was awarded
the Championship. Thesz was defeated by "Whipper" Billy
Watson in Toronto, Ontario, Canada

November 9, 1956 - November 14, 1957 370 days
Thesz defeated "Whipper" Billy Watson in St. Louis, Missouri and
was defeated by Dick Hutton in Toronto, Ontario, Canada

January 24, 1963 - January 7, 1966 1,079 days
Thesz defeated "Nature Boy" Buddy Rogers in Toronto, Ontario,
Canada and was defeated by Gene Kiniski in St. Louis, Missouri.

Dick Hutton
November 14, 1957 - January 9, 1959 421 days
Hutton defeated Lou Thesz in Toronto, Ontario, Canada and was
defeated by Pat O' Connor in St. Louis, Missouri

Pat O' Connor
January 9, 1959 - June 30, 1961 903 days
O'Connor defeated Dick Hutton in St. Louis, Missouri and was
defeated by "Nature Boy" Buddy Rogers in Chicago, Illinois

"Nature Boy" Buddy Rogers
June 30, 1961 - January 24, 1963 573 days
Rogers defeated Pat O' Connor in Chicago, Illinois and was
defeated by Lou Thesz in Toronto, Ontario, Canada. This was a
one fall match, Vince McMahon and his partners did not recognize
the loss for Rodgers and he was declared the first WWWE World
Champion.

Gene Kiniski
January 7, 1966 - February 11, 1969 1,131 days
Kiniski defeated Lou Thesz in St. Louis, Missouri and was
defeated by Dory Funk Jr in Tampa, Florida

Dory Funk Jr.
February 11, 1969 - May 24, 1973 1,563 days
Funk defeated Gene Kiniski in Tampa, Florida and was defeated
by Harley Race in Kansas City, Kansas

Jack Brisco
July 20, 1973 - December 2, 1974 500 days
Brisco defeated Harley Race Houston, Texas and was defeated by
Giant Baba in Kagoshima, Japan

December 9, 1974 - December 10, 1975 366 days
Brisco regained the title defeating Giant Baba in Toyohashi, Japan
and was defeated by Terry Funk in Miami Beach, Florida

Terry Funk
December 10, 1975 - February 6, 1977 424 days
Funk defeated Jack Brisco in Miami Beach, Florida and was
defeated by Harley Race in Toronto, Ontario, Canada

Harley Race
February 6, 1977 - August 21, 1979 926 days
Race defeated Terry Funk in Toronto, Ontario, Canada and was
defeated by "American Dream" Dusty Rhodes in Tampa, Florida

"Nature Boy" Ric Flair
September 17, 1981 - June 10, 1983 631 days
Flair defeated "American Dream" Dusty Rhodes Kansas City,
Kansas and was defeated by Harley Race in St. Louis, Missouri

May 24, 1984 - July 26, 1986 793 days
Flair defeated Kerry Von Erich in Yokosuka, Japan and was
defeated by "American Dream" Dusty Rhodes at The Great
American Bash in Greensboro, North Carolina

August 9, 1986 - September 25, 1987 412 days
Flair defeated "American Dream" Dusty Rhodes in St. Louis,

Missouri and was defeated by "Rugged" Ronnie Garvin in Detroit, Michigan

November 26, 1987 - February 20, 1989 452 days
Flair defeated "Rugged" Ronnie Garvin at Starrcade and was defeated by Ricky "The Dragon" Steamboat at Chi-Town Rumble with both matches taking place in Chicago, Illinois

May 7, 1989 - July 7, 1990 426 days
Flair defeated Ricky "The Dragon" Steamboat at WrestleWar in Nashville, Tennessee and was defeated by Sting The Great American bash in Baltimore, Maryland

From the first day that Flair won the title on September 17, 1981 until he signed with the WWE September 8, 1991 3,644 days had passed, Flair was champion for 3,059 of those days. Which is impressive to say the least. In total Flair held the championship 9 times for a total of 3116 days.

Dan "The Beast" Severn
February 24, 1995 - March 14, 1999 1,479 days
Severn defeated Chris Candido in Erlanger, Kentucky and was defeated by Naoya Ogawa Yokohama, Japan

Blue Demon Jr.
October 25, 2008 - March 14, 2010 505 days
Demon defeated "Scrap Iron" Adam Pearce in Mexico City,
Mexico and was defeated by Pearce in a three way elimination
match that also featured Phil Shatter in Charlotte, North Carolina.
Blue Demon Jr. became the first masked wrestler to win the
championship.

Jax Dane
August 29, 2015 - October 21, 2016 419 days
Dane defeated Hiroyoshi Tenzan in San Antonio, Texas and was
defeated by Tim Storm in Sherman, Texas

Tim Storm
October 21, 2016 - December 9, 2017 414 days
Storm defeated Jax Dane in Sherman, Texas and was defeated by
Nick Aldis at the CZW Cage of Death 19 event in Sewell, New
Jersey

Nick Aldis
October 21, 2018 - current
Aldis defeated Cody Rhodes at the NWA 70th Anniversary Show
in Nashville, Tennessee and as of publication is the current
champion

House Show Title Changes

First published on April 22, 2016 updated as appropriate

With Samoa Joe winning the NXT Championship tonight (April 21, 2016) at the house show in Lowell, Massachusett. A show I wanted to go to but couldn't because of work, but my friends went and now I'm way more jealous than I already was! It led to another buddy and I talking about how there are hardly any title changes on house shows.

Ultimately when you think about house show title changes, one or two always come to mind. Either Diesel beating Bob Backlund for the WWE Championship or Edge defeating Jeff Jarrett for the Intercontinental Championship. It got me wondering just how often it happens?

Obviously back in the day all title changes happened at house shows and never on Television because TV was just a marketing tool to get people to come out to the matches. So the parameters for this list are very simple, the birth of Pay-Per-View. That really changed it all so I'm only counting house show title changes that happened after WrestleMania for WWE and Starrcade 1987 for the NWA/WCW.

I'm counting the NWA / WCW & WWE United States Championship as one title. The WWE & WCW Light-Heavyweight Championships are separate from the WCW / WWE Cruiserweight Championship. With 229 Title Reigns in it's less than four year existence the WWE Hardcore Championship doesn't count. The NWA World Championship is only counted when part of Crockett & WCW as well as TNA. AEW has had no house show title changes. In the end it was longer than I thought it would be, but I have this issue with being thorough.

Active Championships

WWE World Heavyweight Championship

October 12, 1992 Saskatoon, Saskatchewan, Canada
Bret "Hitman" Hart submitted "Nature Boy" Ric Flair - this was Bret's first title run

November 26, 1994 Madison Square Garden
Diesel defeated Bob Backlund who had won the title 3 days prior at Survivor Series

WWE Intercontinental Championship

June 6, 1993 Albany, New York
"Heartbreak Kid" Shawn Michaels defeated Marty Jannetty

May 19, 1995 Montreal, Quebec, Canada
Razor Ramon defeated "Double J" Jeff Jarrett in a ladder match

May 21, 1995 Trois-Rivieres, Quebec, Canada
"Double J" Jeff Jarrett defeated Razor Ramon

August 10, 2003 Des Moines, Iowa
Christian defeated Booker T

WWE / WCW United States Championship

May 22, 1989 Bluefield, West Virginia
"Total Package" Lex Luger defeated Michael "PS" Hayes

August 25, 1991 Atlanta, Georgia
Sting defeated "Stunning" Steve Austin - tournament final for
vacant championship
The title was vacated back July 14th when Lex Luger won the
WCW World Heavyweight Championship at the Great American
Back. Why they held a non-televised tournament I couldn't tell
you.

November 13, 1995 Tokyo, Japan
Kensuke Saski defeated Sting

September 22, 2000 Amarillo, Texas
Terry Funk defeated Lance Storm

September 23, 2000 Lubbock, Texas
Lance Storm defeated Terry Funk - neither title change was
recognized by WCW however WWE does acknowledge them.

July 2, 2017 Madison Square Garden
AJ Styles defeated Kevin Owens

December 26, 2019 Madison Square Garden
Andrade with Zelina Vega defeated Rey Mysterio Jr.

WWE Raw Tag Team Championships

January 15, 2012 Oakland, California
Primo & Epico defeated Air Boom: Evan Bourne & Kofi Kingston

NXT Championship

April 21, 2016 Lowell, Massachusetts
Samoa Joe pinned Finn Balor

NWA World Heavyweight Championship

January 11, 1991 East Rutheford, New Jersey
"Nature Boy" Ric Flair defeated Sting

September 15, 2005 Windsor, Ontario, Canada
Jeff Jarrett defeated Raven

TNA X-Division Championship

September 23, 2010 New York City
Amazing Red defeated Jay Lethal

September 25, 2010 Rahway, New Jersey
Jay Lethal defeated Amazing Red

Inactive Championships

WWE / WCW Cruiserweight Championship

March 20, 1996 Nagoya, Japan
Shinjiro Otani defeated Wild Pegasus (Chris Benoit) tournament
final

March 30, 2000 Baltimore, Maryland
Billy Kidman defeated The Artist

March 31, 2000 Pittsburgh, Pennsylvania
The Artist defeated Billy Kidman

November 15, 2005 Rome, Italy
Nunzio defeated Juventud Guerrera

WWE World Tag Team Championships

February 7, 1992 Denver , Colorado

Money Inc: Ted DiBiase & IRS defeated The Legion of Doom:
Hawk & Animal

July 20, 1992 Worcester, Massachusetts
The Natural Disasters: Earthquake & Typhoon defeated Money
Inc: Ted DiBiase & IRS

June 14, 1993 Columbus, Ohio
The Steiner Brothers: Rick & Scott defeated Money Inc: Ted
DiBiase & IRS

June 16, 1993 Rockford, Illinois
Money Inc: Ted DiBiase & IRS defeated The Steiner Brothers:
Rick & Scott

June 19, 1993 St. Louis, Missouri
The Steiner Brothers: Rick & Scott defeated Money Inc: Ted
DiBiase & IRS

January 17, 1994 Madison Square Garden
The Quebecers: Jacques & Pierre defeated The 1-2-3 Kid & Marty
Jannetty

March 29, 1994 London, England
Men On A Mission: Mo & Mabel defeated The Quebecers:
Jacques & Pierre

March 31, 1994 Sheffield, England
The Quebecers: Jacques & Pierre defeated Men On A Mission: Mo
& Mabel

August 28, 1994 Indianapolis, Indiana
Two Dudes with Attitudes: Diesel & Shawn Michaels defeated
The Headshrinkers

May 19, 1996 Madison Square Garden

The Godwinns: Henry O & Phineas I defeated The Bodydonnas:
Skip & Zip

January 16, 2005 Winnipeg, Manitoba, Canada
La Resistance: Rob Conway & Sylvain Grenier defeated William
Regal & Jonathan Coachman who was substituting for in injured
Eugene

September 5, 2007 Cape Town, South Africa
Paul London & Brian Kendrick defeated Lance Cade & Trevor
Murdoch

September 8, 2007 Johannesburg, South Africa
Lance Cade & Trevor Murdoch defeated Paul London & Brian
Kendrick

December 13, 2008 Hamilton, Ontario, Canada
John Morrison & The Miz defeated CM Punk & Kofi Kingston

WWE Women's Championship

November 25, 1985 Madison Square Garden
The Spider (The Fabulous Moolah) defeated Wendi Richter
July 3, 1986 Brisbane, Australia
Velvet McIntyre defeated The Fabulous Moolah

July 9, 1986 Sydney, Australia
The Fabulous Moolah defeated Velvet McIntyre

July 24, 1987 Houston, Texas
Sensational Sherri defeated The Fabulous Moolah

November 20, 1994 Tokyo Dome
Bull Nakano defeated Alundra Blayze

April 24, 2007 Paris, France
Mickie James defeated Champion: Melina & Victoria in a Threat
Match

Melina defeated Mickie James
Melina was awarded an immediate re-match as Mickie James had
pinned Victoria to win the title

WCW World Heavyweight Championship

January 11, 1991 East Rutheford, New Jersey
"Nature Boy" Ric Flair defeated Sting

December 30, 1992 Baltimore, Maryland
Big Van Vader pinned Ron Simmons

March 11, 1993 London, England
Sting defeated Big Van Vader

March 17, 1993 Dublin, Ireland
Big Van Vader defeated Sting

WCW World Television Championship

January 26, 1988 Raleigh, North Carolina
Mike Rotunda defeated Nikita Koloff

March 31, 1989 Atlanta, Georgia
Sting defeated Mike Rotunda

September 3, 1989 Atlanta, Georgia
The Great Muta defeated Sting for the vacant championship

December 4, 1990 Gainesville, Georgia
The Z-Man defeated "Enforcer" Arn Anderson

January 14, 1991 Marietta, Georgia
"Enforcer" Arn Anderson defeated The Z-Man

February 17, 1996 Baltimore, Maryland
Lex Luger defeated Johnny B. Badd

February 18, 1996 Norfolk, Virginia
Johnny B. Badd defeated Lex Luger

April 30, May 1 - 3, 1998
Chris Benoit & Booker T traded the title back and forth
4/30 Benoit beat Booker Augusta, Georgia
5/1 Booker beat Benoit Greenville, South Carolina
5/2 Benoit beat Booker Charleston, South Carolina
5/3 Booker beat Benoit Savannah, Georgia

WCW Light Heavyweight Championship

December 25, 1991 Atlanta, Georgia
Jushin Thunder Liger defeated Brian Pillman

July 5, 1992 Atlanta, Georgia
Brad Armstrong defeated Scotty Flamingo

WCW World Tag Team Championship

September 10, 1988 Philadelphia, Pennsylvania
The Midnight Express: Bobby Eaton & Stan Lane defeated
"Enforcer" Arn Anderson & Tully Blanchard

October 29, 1988 New Orleans, Louisiana
The Road Warriors: Animal & Hawk defeated The Midnight
Express: Bobby Eaton & Stan Lane

January 16, 1992 Jacksonville, Tennessee
"Enforcer" Arn Anderson & "Beautiful" Bobby Eaton defeated

Ricky "The Dragon" Steamboat & "The Natural" Dustin Rhodes

May 3, 1992 Chicago, Illinois
The Steiner Brothers: Rick & Scott defeated "Enforcer" Arn
Anderson & "Beautiful" Bobby Eaton

July 5, 1992 Atlanta, Georgia
Terry "Bam Bam" Gordy & "Dr. Death" Steve Williams defeated
The Steiner Brothers: Rick & Scott

July 24, 1996 Cincinnati, Ohio
The Steiner Brothers: Rick & Scott defeated Harlem Heat: Booker
T & Stevie Ray

July 27, 1996 Dayton, Ohio
Harlem Heat: Booker T & Stevie Ray defeated The Steiner
Brothers: Rick & Scott

February 12, 2000 Oberhausen, Germany
The Harris Brothers: Ron & Don defeated The Mamalukes: Johnny
The Bull & Big Vito

February 13, 2000 Leipzig, Germany
The Mamalukes: Johnny The Bull & Big Vito defeated The Harris
Brothers: Ron & Don

WCW United States Tag Team Championship

August 24, 1990 East Rutherford, New Jersey
The Steiner Brothers: Rick & Scott defeated The Midnight
Express: Bobby Eaton & Stan Lane

TNA King of the Mountain Championship aka Global & Television

January 27, 2010 Cardiff, Wales
Rob Terry defeated Eric Young

Defunct WWE Championships

Many of us are familiar with Championships that are no longer active in the WWE. You can read about them on their own web page, World Championships, European Championship, World Tag Team Championships, Women's Championship, Light Heavyweight, Cruiserweight, Hardcore, Women's Tag Team Championship, and the Diva's Championship. They even list the WCW World Championship and all the ECW Championships.

However, there are several championships that were created over the years and were only recognized for a short time that the WWE currently doesn't acknowledge their existence.

WWWE United States Tag Team Championships
July 1958 - July 29, 1967

Started in July 1958 as the NWA United States Tag Team Championship for the Capitol Wrestling Corporation with a name change to the WWWE once they left the NWA in April 1963. No reason was given for them being abandoned. You can read the complete title lineage here.

First Champions: Mark Lewin & Don Curtis defeating Hans Schmidt & Dick the Bruiser in a tournament final

Last Champions: Bruno Sammartino & Spiros Arion
Longest Reign: The Fabulous Kangaroos: Al Costello & Roy
Heffernan 409 Days November 28, 1960 - January 11 1962
defeated Johnny Valentine & Chief Big Heart defeated by Buddy
Rogers & Johnny Barend
Most Reigns: Team: The Fabulous Kangaroos: Al Costello & Roy
Heffernan 3 for 514 days, Individual: Dr. Jerry Graham 6 for 632
days

WWWE United States Heavyweight Championship
April 6, 1963 - March 1976

This championship was created after WWWE left the NWA to be
their secondary championship behind the World Championship.
Looking at the title lineage it was pretty much the Bobo Brazil
Championship and I would dispute the authenticity of that final
title run. But then again look at when Duane Gill was the Light
Heavyweight Championship.

First Champion: Bobo Brazil was awarded the Championship upon
its creation
Last Champion: Bobo Brazil
Longest Reign: Bobo Brazil 1837 Days February 19, 1971 - March
1976 was awarded the Championship after Pedro Morales vacated
it when he won the World Championship, title was abandoned.
Most Reigns: Bobo Brazil

WWE North American Heavyweight Championship
February 13, 1979 - April 23, 1981

Only 3 people held the North American Championship with the
longest and last reign belonging to Seiji Sakaguchi at 532 days
until the title was abandoned. Essentially this title was the
precursor to the Intercontinental Heavyweight Championship
which was "won" by Pat Patterson November 1, 1979 while he was
still the North American Heavyweight Champion. The official

WWE History states that on September 1, 1979 Pat Patterson unified his North American Heavyweight Championship with the fictional South American Heavyweight Championship by defeating Johnny Rodz in the equally fictional tournament in Rio De Janeiro, Brazil to be crowned the first ever Intercontinental Champion.

WWWE / WWE International Heavyweight Championship
July 1959 - October 31, 1985

The first time the WWWE or Capitol Wrestling Corporation recognized this title was in July 1959 when Antonio Rocca defeated Buddy Rogers, was later declared inactive in 1963, assuming when WWWE withdrew from the NWA. Revitalized in 1982 and it appears the championship was awarded to Tony Parisi. Akira Maeda defeated Pierre Lefebvre at MSG to be recognized by the WWE. Maeda defended the title in the UWF until July 23 when the WWE and UWF ended their affiliation.
Tatsumi Fujinami defended the Championship in New Japan Pro Wrestling and the WWE for the entirety of his second run with the championship until the companies ended their affiliation. Why the WWE started a second lineage with UWF I couldn't tell you.

WWWE/WWE International Tag Team Championships
June 1, 1969 - January 1, 1972
May 24, 1985 - October 31, 1985

Recognized in the WWWE as a secondary tag team championship but primarily defended in the Pittsburgh Territory. The titles were initially vacated on January 1, 1972 when the territory was sold to the NWF. Later reactivated and recognized in both the WWE and NJPW until their affiliation ended October 31, 1985. These championships were precursor to the IWGP Tag Team Championships that New Japan established December 12, 1985

First Champions: Rising Sons: Toru Tanaka & Mitsu Arakawa
June 1, 1969 awarded championship

Last Champions: Tatsumi Fujinami & Kengo Kimura May 24, 1985 Kobe, Japan defeated Dick Murdoch & Adrian Adonis in tournament final
Longest Reign: The Mongols: Bepo & Geeto 368 days June 15, 1970 - June 18, 1971 defeated Victor Rivera & Tony Marino MSG defeated by Bruno Sammartino & Dominic DeNucci Pittsbugh, PA
Most Reigns: Team: The Mongols 2 for 501 Days, Individual: Geeto Mongol 3 for 515 Days

WWWE Junior Heavyweight Championship
September 1965 - October 31, 1985

The early lineage of the Championship is not exact. Paul DeGalles is the first recognized champion when Toots Mondt, who was a partner with Vince Sr., took over the Pittsburgh Territory as DeGalles has been recognized as the International Junior Heavyweight Champion since July 1960 in West Virginia when Mondt ran that territory.

Title was declared vacant in 1972 when then champion Johnny DeFazio retired. The title was re-established on January 20, 1978 when Carlos Jose Estrada defeated Tony Garea in a tournament final in Uniondale, NY. Three days later at Madison Square Garden Tatsumi Fujinami won the title and took it to New Japan where it was primarily defended until October 31, 1985 when WWE & New Japan ended their affiliation and the title was abandoned. If it was defended in the US it was mostly just at Madison Square Garden. The physical belt that represented this championship was later used as a trophy and presented to "Wild Pegasus" Chris Benoit when he won the 1994 Super-J Cup Tournament. This title was precursor to the IWGP Junior Heavyweight Championship that New Japan established in the summer of 1986.

First Champion: Paul DeGalles September 1965 - October 15, 1965 was defeated by Johnny DeFazio
Last Champion: The Cobra July 28, 1985 - October 31, 1985

defeated Hiro Saito

Longest Reign: Tatsumi Fujinami October 4, 1979 - December 1981 defeated Ryuma Go, vacated the title to move to the heavyweight division.

Most Reigns: Tiger Mask 3 (official) Johnny DeFazio 4 (disputed)

WWE Canadian Championship
August 18, 1985 - January 22, 1986

The WWE had purchased the Montreal based Lutte Internationale promotion and crowned Dino Bravo as the Canadian Champion while they toured Canada. The title was abandoned when Bravo left the promotion making him the only person to hold this Championship.

WWWE / WWE World Martial Arts Heavyweight Championship
December 18, 1978 - 1990

Awarded to Antonio Inoki by Vincent J. McMahon (Sr) upon his debut in the WWE and was recognized by the WWE and NJPW. When the companies parted ways on October 31, 1985 it was then only recognized by NJPW until it was retired in 1990.

The physical belt was then later used in New Japan calling it The Greatest 18 Club Championship and was awarded to Riki Choshu on September 29, 1990, he lost the title to The Great Muta on August 16, 1992 who later retired the title and New Japan abandoned it.

WWE Intercontinental Tag Team Championships
January 7, 1991 - 1991

This championship was created when UWF Japan and WWE started a brief affiliation. The titles were awarded to Perro Aguayo and Gran Hamada who were the only champions when the affiliation ended later in the year.

Of course after I did all this work I found this article on the WWE.com website talking about the 10 Championships You Never Knew Existed in the WWE.

WWE Championships
Defended Outside the WWE

First published on July 9, 2016

It's a very rare occasion when a WWE Championship is defended on a non-promoted WWE event. It has happened but only rarely. For clarifications purposes I am talking about the modern era, essentially from WrestleMania forward. Prior to that, Champions like Bob Backlund and Bruno Sammartino would defend their championships on non-WWE promoted cards.

November 20, 1994 All Japan Women's Pro-Wrestling hosted a supercard entitled Big Egg Wrestling Universe held inside the historic Tokyo Dome with a disputed attendance between 32,000 - 42,000 fans. Either way it's an impressive number for an all girl show featuring 1 male match.

The show consisted of 23 matches featuring multiple promotions including the WWE, and an eight woman Five Star Tournament. This was a truly magnificent show and I would recommend you pick up a copy for yourself. You can find it at IVP video.

In the second to last match on the card, WWE Women's Champion: Alundra Blayze defended against top contender Bull Nakano who at the 9:27 mark pinned Blayze after landing a top rope leg drop to win the Championship.

Bull Nakano would go on to hold the title until April 3, 1995 losing the title back to Blayze at Monday Night Raw the night after WrestleMania XI. Bull Nakano herself would defend the championship at a non-WWE promoted event, AJW's Queendom 1995 defeating Kyoko Inoue.

On November 17, 1998 Duane Gill later Gillberg defeated Christian on Raw in Columbus, Ohio to win the WWE Light-Heavyweight championship and he would hold that title for a record 453 days before dropping the belt to Essa Rios on February 13, 2000 in Austin, TX on Sunday Night Heat.

Duane Gill wrestled in the WWE as enhancement talent from 1991 - 1994. Gill was brought back in for an easy victory for Mankind at the 1998 Survivor Series. After that he joined the JOB Squad and with their help won the championship and was basically never on TV again wrestling only a couple dozen matches on WWE TV until he dropped the title.

However, Gill defended the WWE Light-Heavyweight Championship on numerous Independent Shows including Maryland Championship Wrestling, Steel City Wrestling, World Xtreme Wrestling, and more leagues.

I cannot find any other instances. I know someone might want to say Bret Hart did, but he didn't. True he was the WWE Champion when he wrestled Terry Funk at WrestleFest on September 11, 1997 in Amarillo, Texas however he was never billed as WWE Champion nor brought the belt to the ring.

Update

As United Kingdom Champion Pete Dunne defended the title in several promotions outside of the WWE and NXT brands. He defended the title against Flash Morgan Webster, Joseph Conners, & Jack Gallagher in Progress, against Markus Burke for UCW in Moncton, New Brunswick, Canada and against Zack Gibson at FutureShock Underground in Manchester, England.

WWE's relationship with Evolve grew to having three of their championships defended on Evolve shows. Adam Cole was in two of those matches defending the North American Championship against Walter on June 24, 2018 in Melrose, Massachusetts and the NXT Championship against Akira Tozawa at the 10th Anniversary Show in Philadelphia, Pennsylvania on July 13, 2019. Most recently Drew Gulak successfully defended the Cruiserweight Championship against Kushida in Chicago, Illinois on August 25, 2019.

Champions That Weren't Wrestlers

First published on March 12, 2015

I'm sure everyone remembers the illustrious 12 day reign that David Arquette had as WCW World Champion, but what most may not remember is that he is not the only non-wrestler to win a Championship in one of the major companies. There have been others, and some may even surprise you. My definition of a non-wrestler is someone who may be involved in the wrestling industry but has never been considered a full time competitor or a wrestler in the traditional sense.

David Arquette

On the April 25, 2000 edition of Thunder Arquette pinned fellow non-wrestler Eric Bischoff in a tag team match that also featured Jeff Jarrett and then champion Diamond Dallas Page to win the title. Arquette then turned on Page at Slamboree on May 7, 2000 in a triple cage match to aid Jeff Jarrett in winning his second WCW World Championship.

Judy Bagwell

Rick Steiner and Buff Bagwell won the WCW World Tag Team Championships on October 25, 1998 in Las Vegas at the

WCW Halloween Havoc PPV. During the match Bagwell turned on Steiner and left him on his own, when Steiner won he was allowed to pick his own tag team partner. Initially he chose Kenny Kaos and on the October 26th Nitro in Phoenix they successfully defended the titles against The Giant & Stevie Ray. Shortly thereafter Kaos was injured and Steiner was allowed to choose his next partner. On November 9, 1998 Steiner chose Buff's mother Judy Bagwell to be his partner and she is officially recognized as a WCW World Tag Team Champion.   They never teamed to defend the titles and on January 4, 1999 Steiner was stripped of the titles after he was legitimately injured.

Oklahoma aka Ed Ferrara
     On January 16, 2000 at the Souled Out PPV in Cincinnati, Ohio Oklahoma defeated Madusa to win the WCW Cruiserweight Championship in a 3 minute "match" that was terrible. He was forced to relinquish the championship on the January 19th edition of WCW Thunder for exceeding the weight limit of the title. Wouldn't that have made him ineligible to have a match for the title to begin with?

Eric Bischoff
     On June 5, 2000 at Nitro in Atlanta, Georgia Eric Bischoff defeated Terry Funk for the WCW Hardcore Championship. That just seems wrong to type those words. Granted Bischoff had help from Big Vito, Johnny the Bull and The Cat, but still, wrong. On Thunder that week he awarded the championship to both Big Vito and Johnny the Bull announcing the Freebird rule would be in effect for their joint reign.

Pacman Jones
     At the TNA No Surrender PPV on September 9, 2007 in Orlando, Florida Pacman Jones and Ron Killings defeated Sting and Kurt Angle to win the TNA World Tag Team Championships, yup that is as wrong as it sounds. While on suspension from the NFL Jones and perennial mid-carder Ron Killings beat two of the

all-time greatest wrestlers in Sting and Kurt Angle. Granted Angle attacked Sting which led to the victory, but I mean what else were they supposed to do, Jones was only allowed to appear in a non-physical role. The champs lost their titles to AJ Styles and Tomko at Bound For Glory on October 14th with Consequences Creed wrestling in Jones' place.

Vince McMahon

On September 14, 1999 (aired 9/16) in Las Vegas at a Smackdown taping Mr. McMahon defeated Triple H to win the WWE World Heavyweight Championship with his son Shane McMahon as special guest referee. This was part of the storyline where Triple H drugged and married Stephanie. Mr. McMahon vacated the title on the September 20th RAW in Houston, Texas.

At Backlash in Atlanta, Georgia on April 29, 2007 Mr. McMahon would capture the (WW)ECW Championship defeating champion Bobby Lashley in a handicapped match with partners Shane McMahon and Umaga. He would lose the title back to Lashley in a Street Fight at One Night Stand on June 3rd in Jacksonville, Florida.

Harvey Wippleman

Disguised as Hervina, Harvey Wippleman won a lumberjill snowbunny match on the January 31, 2000 RAW from Pittsburgh to win the WWE Women's Championship. It would be a short reign lasting just 1 day, 3 days in tv time, as Jacqueline would win the title on Smackdown from Detroit, Michigan.

Stephanie McMahon-Helmsley

Stephanie would topple Jacqueline at the March 28, 2000 Smackdown taping in San Antonio, Texas which aired on March 30th to win the Women's Championship. Stephanie would go on to hold the championship for 146 days, not defending it once, until she lost the title to Lita on Raw in Lafayette, Louisiana on August 21, 2000.

Shane McMahon

Of all the McMahon's it can be argued that Shane was a wrestler on the active roster. I even saw him compete in a house show street fight match against Kane at the Cumberland County Civic Center in Portland, Maine. However at the time when he won the European Championship he was not an active wrestler. Shane won the title on February 15, 1999 in Birmingham, Alabama on RAW, pinning X-Pac in a tag team match pitting Shane & Kane vs. Triple H & X-Pac.

Shane did defend the title a few times before retiring the championship on Sunday Night Heat in Uniondale, New York taped March 30, 1999 aired April 4th. On June 21st of that year Shane would award Mideon the Championship after Mideon found it in Shane's duffel bag. The title would be retired for good on July 22, 2002 when it was unified with the Intercontinental Championship.

WWE Hardcore Championship

The hardcore championship changed hands 235 times in its less than 4 year existence before being unified with the Intercontinental Championship. Tommy Dreamer was the last defending champion before losing it to Rob Van Dam. Surprisingly there were only two instances when a non-wrestler won the championship although there were several attempts by non-wrestlers to do so.   Yes Gerald Brisco and Pat Patterson both held the Hardcore Championship but I can't consider then non-wrestlers.

Update

WWE 24/7Championship

The championship was introduced by Mick Foley on May 20, 2019 on Monday Night Raw. Since the title's inception 98 champions (as of publication) have been crowned and among them are six people that are not professional wrestlers. They include Fox Sports commentator Rob Stone, DJ and electronic music producer Marshmello, WWE Senior Account Manager Michael Giaccio, NASCAR driver Kyle Busch, Boston Celtic Enes Kanter, and Rob Gronkowski.

Nicholas Cone

The son of WWE referee John Cone, Nicholas was "randomly" chosen to be Braun Strowman's tag team partner at WrestleMania XXXIV in New Orleans, Louisiana. The duo defeated reigning champions Cesaro & Sheamus, although Strowman dominated the match Nicholas actually tagged in at one point, but quickly tagged out.

The 1993 WWE Women's Championship Tournament

First published July 23, 2018

In December 1993 the WWE announced a tournament would take place to crown a new Women's Champion. The title had been inactive since February 21, 1990 when then champion Rockin' Robin was stripped of the title. She hadn't defended it since June 25, 1989 in Wheeling, West Virginia against Judy Martin.

I had heard about this tournament happening for years but all I even knew were the finals where Alundra Blayze defeated Heidi Lee Morgan to win, but who did they beat to get to the finals? I think most of us know about Madusa aka Alundra Blayze so let's take a look at the other competitors involved in the tournament.

Heidi Lee Morgan

A second generation wrestler, Morgan began her in-ring career in 1987 and was quickly embroiled in a feud in the National Wrestling Federation with Women's Champion Wendi Richter that resulted in the first ever women's cage match on June 20, 1987. Morgan would wrestle matches in NWA, AWA, WCW, and was a co-holder of the LPWA Tag Team Championships with Misty

Blue Simmes. A back injury ended her career in 1997 however she did wrestle in one match in 1999. She is currently a competitive bodybuilder.

Black Venus

Jean Kirkland was trained by the Fabulous Moolah debuting in 1985. She wrestled in the WWE, All Japan Women's Wrestling, NWA, AWA, and later the LPWA from 1990 - 1994. Rumor is that she was in negotiations to be the manager of Harlem Heat in WCW when she passed away. Kirkland died September 30, 1995.

Rusty Thomas

Also known as Rusty Foxx I can't find a lot of information on her but this is what I have. She debuted in 1988 and wrestled for the WWE, WWWA, and several independent promotions. She held a few indie Women's Championships including National Wrestling League, Mid-Eastern Championship Wrestling and others. I saw her wrestle live once in Livermore Falls, Maine on November 13, 1998 for Eastern Wrestling Alliance. She battled Malia Hosaka to a no contest when they both brawled in and out of the ring and the referee threw the match out.

Angie Marino

I cannot find any information about Marino, in fact this is the only match I can find on record for her anywhere on the internet.

The Tournament

November 29, 1993 Memphis, Tennessee Mid-South Coliseum

USWA - Tournament Match for the WWE Women's Championship
Madusa defeated Alison Royal

November 30, 1993 Springfield, Massachusetts

Dark Matches - First Round
Heidi Lee Morgan defeated Black Venus
Rusty Thomas defeated Angie Marino

December 1, 1993 Utica, New York

Dark Match - Semi Final
Heidi Lee Morgan defeated Rusty Thomas

December 13, 1993 Poughkeepsie, New York

All American Wrestling taping aired December 26, 1993
Finals: Alundra Blayze defeated Heidi Lee Morgan with a German
Suplex to win the championship

Originally it appeared as though the tournament took place
over three nights with Blayze getting a bye to the finals of the
tournament. Heidi Lee Morgan had to win two matches on
consecutive nights to advance to the finals. I later found that
Blayze, under the name Madusa, wrestled an opening round match
in the USWA: United States Wrestling Association. That still
leaves her either getting a first or second round bye to the finals.

It surprises me that four of the five matches were dark
matches and even the final wasn't aired live on Raw but instead on
the B weekend show All American Wrestling. You would think if
they really wanted to build the division it would have been more
prominent.

The 1990 WWE Intercontinental Championship Tournament

First published August 7, 2018

April 14, 1990 Superstars of Wrestling in an Update segment WWE President Jack Tunney announced that after winning the WWE Championship at WrestleMania VI The Ultimate Warrior is surrendering the Intercontinental Championship. The new champion would be decided in a tournament.

April 4, 1990 Glen Falls, New York Wrestling Superstars Taping

Aired April 28th
Round 1: Tito Santana defeated Akeem The African Dream by count out when Santana's flying forearm knocked Akeen out of the ring

Aired May 5th
Round 1: Mr. Perfect pinned Jimmy Snuka with his feet on the ropes

April 23, 1990 Austin, Texas Wrestling Superstars Taping

Aired May 12th
Round 1: Dino Bravo with Jimmy Hart wrestled Brutus Beefcake
to a double count out

Aired May 19th
Finals: Mr. Perfect pinned Tito Santana with an inside cradle after
being distracted by Bobby "The Brain" Heenan, after the match it
was announced that Heenan was Mr. Perfect's new manager

April 24, 1990 San Antonio, Texas Wrestling Challenge Taping

Aired May 13th
Round 1: "Rowdy" Roddy Piper and Rick Martel to a double
disqualification when Martel used his Arrogance atomizer and
Piper used a steel chair.

You did not read that wrong. Two of the opening round
matches ended with both men being eliminated from the
tournament. Not only that but the finals and a new champion was
declared before the final first round match even took place.

Rey Mysterio Jr
The Weakest World Champion

First published October 20, 2017

At WrestleMania 22, April 2, 2006, in Chicago Rey Mysterio Jr. defeated Randy Orton and World Heavyweight Champion: Kurt Angle in nine and a half minutes to win the World Heavyweight Championship. I was not happy at all! I was pissed when Mysterio won the Royal Rumble because for 60 of the 62 minutes he was in the ring he hid in the corner avoiding competition, if you're a heel that's smart, if you're the underdog babyface you look weak.

Mysterio winning the championship was the feel good moment stemming from the unfortunate death of Eddie Guerrero the previous November. My thought is that it should have been Chavo, an actual Guerrero family member to win the championship in Eddie's honor.

I am of the opinion that Mysterio was booked as the weakest World Champion in recent history and it began before he won the Championship. After winning the Rumble Mysterio was goaded into putting his WrestleMania title match on the line against Randy Orton at the No Way Out pay-per-view in Baltimore on February 19th. A match that Mysterio lost. Teddy Long, the SmackDown general manager then re-inserted Mysterio in the match making it a Triple Threat. He lost the match that he "earned" and then was awarded for no reason and put back in the match.

Mysterio's title reign lasted 112 days from WrestleMania April 2, 2006 to July 23, 2006 at the Great American Bash, where he lost the championship to King Booker. He competed in 48 matches during that period, sixteen of those were broadcast on television or PPV; the rest were at house shows. Of those sixteen matches only six of those did he win clean in the ring. Of the ten remaining one was a tag match that his team won and one was a dq victory. The remaining eight saw him come out on the losing end. Mysterio's second reign as World Champion only got worse.

Lasting 28 days from June 20, 2010 to July 18, 2010 he competed in only thirteen matches of which three were televised. He teamed with Big Show, defeating Cody Rhodes & Jack Swagger by disqualification. Then on July 18th at the Money in the Bank pay-per-view he defeated Jack Swagger in about ten minutes to retain the title only to have Kane cash in his Money in the Bank losing the title in less than a minute.

Mysterio has had one reign as WWE Champion holding the title for only a couple hours. On July 25, 2011 on Monday Night Raw from Hampton, Virginia Mysterio defeated Miz in the finals of a tournament to be declared the new champion. John Cena challenged Mysterio to a match that night and defeated Mysterio for the championship.

It's no secret to my friends that I am not a fan of Rey Mysterio, but it wasn't always that way. Essentially I still am a fan of anything he did prior to being unmasked in WCW, after that though, pass. Me being a fan of Mysterio or not though doesn't change the fact that in my opinion as World Champion he was made to look like a fool.

Pete Dunne
The Longest Reigning WWE Champion in 30 Years

First published on October 26, 2018 updated as appropriate

At 685 days former NXT United Kingdom Champion "Brusierweight" Pete Dunne has become the longest continuous reigning singles champion in over 30 years since Hulk Hogan's first title reign came to an end on February 5, 1988.

Dunne represented the WWE's United Kingdom brand but unlike other champions in the WWE, Dunne defended his championship in promotions around the world. As champion Dunne competed in over 200 matches. While not all were title matches compare that to Brock Lesnar who wrestled just 17 matches in his 504 day reign as Universal Champion and Asuka who wrestled 149 matches in her 523 day reign as NXT Women's Champion.

In the near 67 year history of the WWE Pete Dunne ranks sixth on the list of longest single reigning champions. That is not an accomplishment that you can dismiss as only Bruno Sammartino, Bob Backlund, Hulk Hogan, and Pedro Morales have had a longer continuous single reign as a champion.

Here are the 15 longest single reigning champions in WWE History:

2,803 Days Bruno Sammartino WWWE World Heavyweight Champion May 17, 1963 - January 18, 1971

2,135 Days Bob Backlund WWE World HeavyweightChampion February 20, 1978 - December 26, 1983

1,474 Days Hulk Hogan WWE World Heavyweight Champion January 23, 1984 - February 5, 1988

1,237 Days Bruno Sammartino WWE World Heavyweight Champion December 10, 1973 - April 30, 1977

1,027 Days Pedro Morales WWWE World Heavyweight Champion February 20, 1978 - December 1, 1973

685 Days Pete Dunne WWE United Kingdom Champion May 20, 2017 - April 5, 2019

523 Days Lex Luger WCW United States Champion May 22, 1989 - October 27, 1990

523 Days Asuka NXT Women's Champion April 1, 2016 - September 6, 2017

504 Days Brock Lesnar WWE Universal Champion April 2, 2017 - August 19, 2018

502 Days Rockin' Robin WWE Women's Champion October 7, 1988 - February 21, 1990

454 Days Honky Tonk Man WWE Intercontinental Heavyweight Champion June 2, 1987 -
August 29, 1988

448 Days Trish Stratus WWE Women's Champion January 9, 2005 - April 2, 2006

448 Days Duane Gill WWE Light Heavyweight Champion November 17, 1998 - February 8, 2000

441 Days Sensational Sherri WWE Women's Champion July 24, 1987 - October 7, 1988

434 Days CM Punk WWE Champion November 20, 2011 - January 27, 2013

For those wondering I didn't count The Fabulous Moolah's 10,170 days reign as Women's Champion because even though the WWE does officially recognize it, as it was the NWA Women's Championship until May 19, 1984 when it was renamed the WWE Women's Championship. There is a lot of controversy surrounding the actual length of the reign and the number of times the lost it officially or otherwise until Wendi Richter defeated her for it on July 23, 1984.

Other former championships I didn't include because they were only recognized occasionally were the WWWE United States Heavyweight Championship (1963 - 1976), WWE International Championship (1959 - 1984), WWE Junior Heavyweight Championship (1965 - 1985), WWE World Martial Arts Heavyweight Championship (1978 - 1989) and all WCW & ECW Championships.

The Many Champions of "Captain" Lou Albano

First published April 9, 2017

It has been debated for years as to who is the greatest wrestling manager of all time. Both Jim Cornette and Paul Heyman, both outstanding managers themselves, have said that Bobby "The Brain" Heenan is. And while I don't disagree with that sentiment however, an argument could be made that "Captain" Lou Albano is the greatest of all time.

Dubbed "The Guiding Light" Albano mentored thirteen different tag teams to a combined 15 WWWE/WWE Tag Team Championships. He also was the man who brought Ivan Koloff in to challenge and defeat Bruno Sammartino for his WWWE World Championship ending Sammartino's near 8 year reign as champion. Also he seconded both Magnificent Muraco and Greg "The Hammer" Valentine when they captured the WWE Intercontinental Championship.

Albano himself is a former WWWE United States Tag Team Champion, winning the title on July 10, 1967 with partner Tony Altimore as The Sicilians. It has been credited to Bruno Sammartino and Vince McMahon Sr for pushing Albano toward becoming a manager. They both felt that his in ring work was lacking whereas his gift of gab made him stand out among his

peers.
Let's breakdown who his chargers were and when they won the championship:

WWWE World Heavyweight Championship

Ivan Koloff
January 18, 1971 Madison Square Garden defeated Bruno Sammartino

WWE Intercontinental Championship

Magnificent Muraco
January 22, 1983 Madison Square Garden defeated Pedro Morales

Greg "The Hammer" Valentine
September 24, 1984 London, Ontario defeated Tito Santana

WWWE/WWE World Tag Team Championships

"Crazy" Luke Graham & Tarzan Tyler
June 3, 1971 New Orleans, LA defeated Dick The Bruiser & The Sheik in a tournament final to become the first ever champions

Baron Mike Scicluna & King Curtis Iaukea
February 1, 1972 Philadelpha, PA defeated Karl Gotch & Rene Goulet

The Valiant Brothers: Jimmy & Johnny
May 8, 1974 Hamburg, PA defeated Tony Garea & Dean Ho

The BlackJacks: BlackJack Lanza & BlackJack Mulligan
August 26, 1975 Philadelphia, PA defeated Dominic DeNucci & Pat Barrett

The Executioners: 1 & 2 (Killer Kowalski & Big John Studd)

May 11, 1976 Philadelphia, PA defeated Louis Cerdan & Tony Parisi

The Yukon Lumberjacks: Yukon Eric & Yukon Pierre
June 26, 1978 New York, NY defeated Dino Bravo & Dominic DeNucci

The Valiant Brothers: Jerry & Johnny
March 6, 1979 Allentown, PA defeated Tony Garea & Larry Zbyszko

The Wild Samoans: Afa & Sika
April 12, 1980 Philadelphia, PA defeated Ivan Putski & Tito Santans

September 9, 1980 Philadelphia, PA defeated Tony Garea & Rene Goulet in tournament final

The Moondogs: King, Rex, & Spot
March 17, 1981 Allentown, PA defeated Tony Garea & Rick Martel
Rex & King won the titles 45 days into the reign Spot replaced King on the team as champion

Mr. Fuji & Mr. Saito
October 13, 1981 Allentown, PA defeated Tony Garea & Rick Martel

The Wild Samoans: Afa & Sika
March 8, 1983 Allentown, PA defeated Chief Jay & Jules Strongbow

The U.S. Express: Mike Rotundo & Barry Windham
January 21, 1985 Hartford, CT defeated The North-South Connection: Adrian Adonis & Dick Murdoch

The British Bulldogs: Dynamite Kid & Davey Boy Smith
April 7, 1986 WrestleMania 2 Rosemont, IL defeated The Dream
Team: Brutus Beefcake & Greg "The Hammer" Valentine

The Headshrinkers: Samu & Fatu
April 26, 1994 Burlington, VT defeated The Quebecers: Pierre &
Jacques

WWWE/WWE International Tag Team Championships

The Mongols: Bepo & Geeto
June 15, 1970 New York, NY defeated Bruno Sammartino & The
Battman
Albano bought The Mongols contract from Tony Angelo after they
had won the titles

Albano's resume of champions is extremely impressive,
and I believe that no other manager has managed so many different
champions as the Captain. Whether this qualifies him as the
greatest of all time or not, I'm not sure, but you cannot overlook
what an outstanding accomplishment this is.

The Natural Disasters
Tag Team Champions?

First published January 2, 2017

During a recent episode of my wrestling podcast Podcast of 1,000 Holds it was brought up about the Natural Disasters: Earthquake & Typhoon being Tag Team Champions and I refuted it because I honestly had no memory of them wearing the gold. My buddy Roy brought it to my attention that they did in fact hold the titles. So, I did a quick search and sure enough in 1992 they held the titles for 85 days. Because of my error in knowledge I'm dedicating a blog post to the former Tag Team Champions.

Earthquake, John Tenta, joined the WWE in 1989 initially as the Canadian Earthquake before dropping the geographical location from his name. In 1990 he began a feud with Hulk Hogan culminating at SummerSlam 1990 where Hogan won by count-out. Typhoon, Fred Ottman, also joined the WWE in the summer of 1989 working house shows until he TV debut in 1990 as Tugboat. He would eventually team with Hogan in tag matches against Earthquake and Dino Bravo.

Tugboat turned heel in June 1991 deserting The Bushwhackers in a six man tag team match against The Nasty Boys and Earthquake. Shortly thereafter he would change his name to Typhoon and join forces with Earthquake as The Natural

Disasters.

Their first big match was at SummerSlam 1991 where they defeated The Bushwhackers who had Andre the Giant in their corner. Post match they advanced on Andre but were stopped by the Legion of Doom. They began a feud with Hawk & Animal that led to a Championship match at Royal Rumble 1992 that the Natural Disasters won by count out.

This victory lead to their eventual face turn as their manager "The Mouth of the South" Jimmy Hart used their guaranteed for his other team of Money Inc: "Million Dollar Man" Ted DiBiase & IRS who defeated the Legion of Doom for the Tag Team Championships February 7, 1992 at a house show in Denver, Colorado.

The Natural Disasters defeated Money Inc by count out at WrestleMania VIII and won many matches by DQ on the house show loop. Finally on July 20, 1992 in Worcester, Massachusetts in Superstars TV taping dark match they defeated Money Inc for the tag team championships. Over the next 85 days they defended the titles at house shows against Money Inc then later The Beverly Brothers: Beau & Blake, while squashing jobbers on TV.

The only pay-per-view match as champions was at SummerSlam 1992 at Wembley Stadium in London, England against The Beverly Brothers. This is also the only match on the WWE Network with them as champs. I recently re-watched this match and it was terrible, just awful. However, the fans were popping huge for them. I truly cannot believe it or understand why. I guess wrestling was simpler then, people cheered for the good guys and booed the bad guys.

On October 13, 1992 in Regina, Saskatchewan, Canada Money Inc defeated The Natural Disasters to win the titles in a match that aired November 1st on Wrestling Challenge. The Disasters would win several house show matches but never regained the gold.

Their last match as a team in the WWE was a house show loss to the Headshrinkers: Fatu & Samu on December 12, 1992 in San Diego, California. At the Royal Rumble in 1993 Typhoon entered at number 21 and when Earthquake entered at number 23 he attacked his partner eliminating him.

There was no follow up to their dissolved partnership as Tenta would leave the WWE in 1993 then return for a Sumo feud with Yokozuna in 1994 before joining WCW later that year. Ottman would join WCW in 1993 as the Shockmaster.

Ottman and Tenta would team up one more time as The Natural Disasters in a six man tag April 29, 2000 at a Future of Wrestling show where they teamed with Bobby Rogers in a losing effort to Larry Lane & The Suicidal Tendencies Dennis & Sean Allen.

Bonus:

Super World of Sports was a wrestling promotion in Japan that was started in 1990 by Genichiro Tenryu and they had a working relationship with the WWE before folding in mid-1992. On April 17, 1992 in Yokohama, Japan The Natural Disasters defeated George & Shunji Takano to win the SWS Tag Team Championships. They would lose the titles the next day on April 18th to King Haku & Yoshiaki Yatsu in Tokyo.

The Headbangers
WWE Team Champions?

First published on March 24, 2019

I pride myself on my wrestling knowledge and considering I was eighteen in 1997 during one of the hottest years in wrestling I can't believe I forgot this, but The Headbangers were the WWE Team Champions!

I remember them winning the NWA Tag Team Championships, they were champions from February 17 - March 30, 1998, and their feud with the Oddities over the Tag Team Champions of the Universe foam belts. But, I have no recollection of them holding the WWE Tag Team gold until listening to a recent episode of Something to Wrestle.

On September 7, 1997 in Louisville, Kentucky at In Your House: Ground Zero the Headbangers won a fatal four way match for the vacant Tag Team Championships. They were the clear underdogs in the match with opponents The Godwinns, The Legion of Doom, and Owen hart & The British Bulldog I'm sure no one expected the Headbangers to win.

The months leading up to the PPV the Headbangers were on a tremendous losing streak at house shows and on television primarily against The Godwinns. After winning the championships they didn't start out well losing to the Godwinns in three minutes the next night on Raw in a non-title match.

On TV they would feud with The Godwinns and their new manager Cletus, but pick up wins on the house shows first against Rocky Maivia & Kama and later Savio Vega & Miguel Perez Jr. Their biggest win as champions came on September 20, 1997 in Birmingham, England at the One Night Only PPV where they defeated Savio Vega & Miguel Perez Jr. at 13:34 with the Bombs Away on Perez.

Their twenty eight day reign came to an end in St. Louis, Missouri at In Your House: Badd Blood on October 5, 1997 when the Godwinns won the championships when Phinneas pinned Mosh. The Headbangers would beat the Godwinns in a non-title lumberjack match the next night on Raw, however the Godwinns would lose the championship to the Legion of Doom October 7th. The Headbangers never recaptured the WWE Tag Team championships, however they did win several regional tag team championships over the years. 2019 marked their 25th year teaming together.

I've seen the Headbangers live three times:

March 29, 1998 WrestleMania XIV, Boston, Massachusetts
The Headbangers were in the opening 15 team battle royal that was eventually won by LOD 2000.

April 26, 2012 Live Pro Wrestling, Waterville, Maine
CCW Tag Team Champions: The Headbangers: Mosh & Thrasher defeated The Prestige: Ryan Waters & Matt Magnum with the Stage Dive on Waters.

March 7, 2015 Boston Pro Wrestling Marathon Day 2, Abington, Massachusetts
Falls Count Anywhere: "Real Deal" Brandon Locke w/ Adam Barisano pinned "Taskmaster" Kevin Sullivan after the match Sullivan beat up Barisano and then the Headbangers: Mosh &

Thrasher attacked Barisano attempting the Stage Dive but Barisano botched it. The Headbangers were supposed to wrestle on Day 3 of the Boston Pro Wrestling Marathon but the promoter cancelled the final day of the show at the last minute.

At both the show in 2012 & 2015 I chatted with them and got some cards signed. They were super cool to talk to and were genuinely nice guys.

Jerry Lynn was the WWE Light Heavyweight Champion?

First published on November 5, 2018

Listening to the Mikey Whipwreck and Jerry Lynn's new podcast the other day it was mentioned by the host that Lynn was a former WWE Light Heavyweight Champion. This statement gave me pause because I didn't remember Lynn being champion straight away so I decided to look into it.
On April 29, 2001 from Chicago on a live Sunday Night Heat before the Backlash Pay Per View Lynn made his WWE television debut defeating Light Heavyweight Champion: Crash Hardy to win the championship in about three and a half minutes.

This match was after the closure of WCW & ECW and even though Lynn was in the WWE during the invasion angle he was not affiliated with the ECW brand during this time. This was Lynn's 4th run with the promotion after brief stints in 1989, 1995, & 1997.

He debuted on March 25th at a house show in Baltimore defeating Essa Rios. He wrestled several house shows leading up to his match with Holly including pinning Brian Danielson at the now TD Garden in Boston on April 9th in a dark match.
He defended the title for 37 days after winning the championship against: Kevin Kruger, Grandmaster Sexay, Crash Holly, Taka

Michinoku, Essa Rios, Dean Malenko, Christopher Daniels, Eddie Guerrero, Funaki, and Michael Shane before his loss to Jeff Hardy. Following the loss he had one rematch and then continued wrestling essentially the same core guys. He made his Madison Square Garden debut on June 25th defeating Essa Rios with a tornado DDT in five and a half minutes on a taped Jakked that aired on June 30th.

On July 31st in Washington DC he wrestled Hardcore Champion: Rob Van Dam in a short match losing to the five star frog splash that was not anywhere near to the level of their matches from ECW. This was the only significant match of Lynn's that I remembered from this run and it was a bit of a disappointment considering their history.

His final match was one week later on August 6th defeating Justin Incredible on a match taped for Jakked. During his short run he wrestled primarily on Jakked with a couple matches on Raw and SmackDown and had no in-ring PPV appearances. At Judgement Day on May 20th he was relegated to making an appearance at WWE New York.

Lynn would go on to have a great career in TNA, Ring of Honor, and on the indies wrestling his last match March 23, 2013 in Minneapolis defeating Horace the Psychopath, JB Trask, & Sean Waltman in a Fatal Four Way.

I had the pleasure of meeting Jerry Lynn just one time on September 5, 2009 in Fairfield, Maine for the indie promotion Pro Wrestling America. This show had only 10 fans in attendance and the majority of the wrestlers cancelled or no showed because a rival promotion about an hour north was also running.

Both Mr. Lynn and Sonjay Dutt were booked for both shows. They worked the first half of the show in Brewer and then drove down to this show. The first half of our show consisted of four shit-tastic matches with all trainees. One match was a Sack of Tacks match where no one took a bump in the tacks.

Finally, Lynn and Dutt arrived and tore the house down! Lynn pinned Champion: Mark Moment with the cradle piledriver and in the main event in falls count anywhere match Cameron

Matthews pinned Dutt with a piledriver.

Update

Since this post I met Jerry Lynn again on Friday April 5, 2019 at WrestleCon in New York City! My buddies Jay, Mikey, & I went down for WrestleMania Weekend but didn't go to any WWE events instead hitting WrestleCon and the New Japan show at Madison Square Garden. Jerry Lynn was a guest at WrestleCon and I had him sign a WWE card to complete my Jerry Lynn collection. At the show ten years ago he signed a TNA & ECW card for me.

Ric Flair's Intercontinental Championship Reign

First published on August 17, 2018

"Nature Boy" Ric Flair is one of the greatest wrestlers in the history of professional wrestling and has always been one of my all time favorites. I have had the pleasure of meeting Mr. Flair on a few occasions and I wrote about it here.

Through-out his career Mr. Flair has held more championships beyond being a 16 time World Heavyweight Champion. He held numerous titles in Mid-Atlantic Wrestling & Jim Crockett Promotions and the NWA Missouri Heavyweight Championship.

In September 2005 Flair had been back in the WWE for almost three years, in that time he had two Tag Team title runs with Batista but his last singles reign as a champion had been five and half years earlier in WCW with a controversial day as Heavyweight Championship. At age 56 many thought Flairs days were coming to an end, and as much as I'd hoped for one more World Championship run, his days as a champion were over.

On September 5th in Oklahoma City at the Unforgiven PPV "Nature Boy" Ric Flair opened the show against Carlito in a match for the Intercontinental Championship. This match was set up on an edition of Carlito's Cabana where Flair was the guest and

Carlito spit an apple in Flair's face before the two came to blows. Back in early 1983 Flair wrestled Carlos Colon, Carlito's father, in a controversial series of matches where Colon allegedly won and lost the NWA World Championship to Flair in a change that was never recognized by the NWA. On this night though in just over eleven and a half minutes and much to the surprise of those in attendance Flair submitted Carlito with his figure four leg lock to capture the championship.

Near the end of this match Flair went to the top and Carlito caught him for the usual bodyslam off the top rope, but Flair punched him and then came off with a blow to Carlito's head. The crowd popped big time and Flair raised his arms in victory, it was quite a funny moment. The crowd erupted for the tap out! Post match Flair cut a promo about how proud he was to win this prestigious championship. That it was just as sweet as winning each of those 16 world championships.

The next night on Raw in Wichita Falls, Texas Flair would retain the title in just over 20 minutes in a rematch with Carlito winning by submission with the figure four leg lock. Flair would then begin a five month run as champion, some would say his most successful run in the WWE seconded only by his final Career Threatening run in 2007 / 2008.

He wrestled on the house shows defending the title against first Carlito and then Triple H and finally against Shelton Benjamin before losing the championship to Benjamin on the February 20, 2006 Monday Night Raw in Trenton, New Jersey. All the time he feuded on television with Triple H and Edge. His biggest defense of this run came in San Diego at Taboo Tuesday on November 1st in a steel cage match with Triple H. The build for this match was excellent with Hunter turning on Flair in a tag team match and busting him open with a sledge hammer shot. Flair begged the fans to vote for a cage match between himself and Triple H at the PPV and got his wish.

The promo package played prior to this match was tremendous. Flair came out second to a huge ovation from the crowd. When I think of Ric Flair what comes to mind is the Four

Horsemen, the NWA Championship, and his famous bloody steel cage battles for that championship. This match hearkened back to those matches as both men were busted open and Flair blonde hair was soaked red with blood.

The match opened quickly with both men trading blows and Flair lighting up Triple H's chest with chops. Hunter then took over for several minutes sending Flair into the cage opening him up just a few minutes into the match.
Eventually Flair took over and sent Triple H into the busting open The Game and dominated the rest of the match. The finish came when Flair pulled a chair into the ring and laid Triple H out with it. He then escaped the cage getting the victory in just under 24 minutes.

I had the opportunity to see Flair live as Intercontinental Champion at a live Monday Night Raw from TD Garden in Boston on December 12, 2005. In an Elimination Chamber qualifying match Kurt Angle defeated Flair with the ankle lock. Sadly none of my pictures that I took with Flair wearing the belt came out well.

Flair's final championship would come one year later on November 5, 2006 at the now renamed Cyber Sunday. Ric Flair and "Rowdy" Roddy Piper would defeat Spirit Squad members Kenny & Mikey to win the WWE Tag Team Championships. They would lose the titles eight days later at Raw from Manchester, England to Rated-RKO: Edge & Randy Orton. After winning the titles Flair and Piper teamed with the Highlanders for five, eight man tag matches against The Spirit Squad across the United Kingdom.

"Million Dollar Man" Ted DiBiase: WWE Champion?

First published on July 21, 2016

I remember it vividly, February 5, 1988 I'm 8 years old my cousins are over and we are all in my brothers room watching The Main Event on NBC and I'm positive that Hulk Hogan is going to vanquish Andre the Giant and again retain the WWE World Heavyweight Championship!

But then the unthinkable happens he loses. But his shoulder was up!! According to Jesse Ventura, the evil Ted DiBiase paid someone to have plastic surgery to look like the referee to cheat Hogan out of his championship! I was literally devastated and the rest of my evening was ruined.

Shortly after "winning" the championship Andre surrendered it to villainous Ted DiBiase making him an unworthy champion. This travesty of justice was rectified when on February 13th on Superstars of Wrestling President Jack Tunney declared the championship vacant. As we all know a tournament was held at WrestleMania IV "Macho Man" Randy Savage defeated DiBiase in the finals to win his first championship.

In the official history of the WWE World Heavyweight Championship on WWE.com Andre won the title on February 5th and was champion for 59 minutes. WWE doesn't officially recognize DiBiase as champion however for at least four shows DiBiase was recognized as champion and came to the ring with the championship belt.

Thanks to the website The History of WWE here are those matches:

February 6, 1988 Boston Garden, Massachusetts matinee show
Televised on NESN - included Craig DeGeorge & Lord Alfred Hayes on commentary
Hulk Hogan & Bam Bam Bigelow with Sir Oliver Humperdink defeated Ted Dibiase with Virgil & Andre the Giant at 7:59 when Hogan pinned Dibiase with the leg drop after Andre's arm became entangled in the ring ropes; prior to the bout, Dibiase came to the ring wearing the WWE World Title belt and was introduced as the new champion as a result of what occured the previous night in Indianapolis

February 6, 1988 Philadelphia Spectrum, Pennsylvania evening show
Televised on the PRISM Network - featured Dick Graham & Lord Alfred Hayes on commentary
Hulk Hogan & Bam Bam Bigelow with Sir Oliver Humperdink defeated Andre the Giant & Ted Dibiase with Virgil at 9:56 when Hogan pinned Dibiase with the leg drop after Andre became tied in the ring ropes; prior to the bout, Dibiase came to the ring in possession of the world title belt and was announced as the champion

February 7, 1988 San Diego, California
Ted Dibiase defeated Bam Bam Bigelow; Dibiase was recognized as WWE World Champion for the bout

February 8, 1988 Los Angeles, California
Ted Dibiase pinned Bam Bam Bigelow after Virgil hit Bigelow with the world title belt; Dibiase was billed as the WWE World Champion and the match was recognized as a title match

Antonio Inoki WWE Champion?

First published on March 9, 2018

If you go to Wikipedia under the List of WWE Champions section it notates that on November 30, 1979 in Tokushima, Japan Antonio Inoki defeated Bob Backlund to win the WWE Championship. It goes on to say that on December 6, 1979 in Tokyo Inoki vacated the title after a rematch with Backlund that ended in a no contest when Tiger Jeet Singh interfered. Finally it states that Backlund regained the vacated title when he defeated Bobby Duncum in a Texas Death Match on December 17, 1979 at Madison Square Garden. Of course the WWE does not recognize this title change in their official championship lineage.

These types of phantom title changes happened frequently in the NWA however this is the only known incident in the WWE. Recently I subscribed to New Japan World and while searching their archivesI found these controversial matches and had to watch them.

The match itself isn't anything exciting by today's standards but was very good for back then. The match is about thirty minutes long and as it nears the end Tiger Jeet Singh is seen being held at ringside by the young boys. Inoki goes over and yells at Singh and while distracted Backlund hits his finisher, the dreaded atomic drop and gets the three count.

I watched it twice, the referee clearly counts three but

doesn't call for the bell or anything. Backlund jumps up and throws his fist in the air thinking he has won when Inoki grabs him and nails a side suplex and goes for the cover.

Backlund appears to kick out just as the referee counts three but the bell immediately rings and the commentators start yelling in Japanese but you can hear "WWE Champion" clearly. The ring fills up with wrestlers moments after the bell rings and Inoki is raised up on their shoulders. Tiger Jeet Singh gets in the ring where Backlund attacks him followed by Inoki. Eventually Singh is cleared out of the ring and they have the ceremony where they put the championship on Inoki and give him a large trophy. Backlund grabs the mic and says that the referee counted three. It appears as though they screwed Backlund out of the championship but it also appears as though it was a work.

This match was the first day of the tour that Backlund was on. Over the next few days he worked matches getting wins over Seiji Sakaguchu, Tiger Jeet Singh, and Tatsumi Fujinami. On December 3, 1979 Backlund teamed with Pedro Morales to defeat Antonio Inoki and Tatsumi Fujimani.

December 6, 1979 was the return title match and this too is on New Japan World. In my opinion this match is better than the one a week prior. The finish of this match comes when Inoki has Backlund in a short arm scissors and Backlund picks him up carrying him to the corner and dumping him over the top rope. Tiger Jeet Singh runs out and goes to attack Inoki on the floor but Inoki defends himself. Once back on the apron Backlund lifts Inoki in the Atomic Drop position and with the referee distracted by Singh Backlund crotches Inoki on the top rope and pins him for a three count.

The referee gives Backlund the championship and declares him the winner. However it appears as though the New Japan officials are going to overturn the referees decision much to the chagrin of Backlund and the referee. For several minutes they talk to Backlund, I have no idea what they are saying. Backlund just keeps walking up and down the apron shaking his head and yelling no. He threatens to hit them with the Championship belt several times. Eventually they get the belt away from Backlund and the clip ends with them giving the belt to Inoki.

Three days later on December 9th, Backlund billed as WWE Champion lost to Intercontinental Champion Pat Patterson by count-out in Toronto at Maple Leaf Gardens. Eight days later at Madison Square Garden Backlund defeated Bobby Duncum in the Texas Death Match.

In his book "Backlund" Bob Backlund wrote that the switch was done as a favor to Inoki to keep him on par with his rival Giant Baba of All Japan Pro Wrestling had already had two short runs with the NWA World Heavyweight Championship defeating Jack Brisco in 1974 and Harley Race in 1979.

The Year the WCW World Championship Changed Hands 25 Times

First published May 7, 2017

That's right in the year 2000, the final full year the promotion was in operation, the WCW World Heavyweight Championship changed hands or was vacated 25 times. Is it any wonder why this promotion ultimately folded.

1) January 16, 2000 Cincinnati, Ohio Souled Out
Bret Hart is forced to vacate the title due to injury after being kicked in the head and being concussed by Goldberg

2) January 16, 2000 Cincinnati, Ohio Souled Out
Chris Benoit defeated Sid Vicious with Arn Anderson as the special guest referee

3) January 17, 2000 Columbus, Ohio Nitro
Title is vacated: storyline Arn Anderson states he was forced to reverse the decision because Sid's leg was under the rope when he submitted to the crossface. In reality Benoit left the WCW with Eddie Guerrero, Dean Malenko, & Perry Saturn

4) January 24, 2000 Los Angeles, California Nitro
Sid Vicious defeated Kevin Nash for the vacant championship. He had to defeated The Harris Brothers in a handicapped match for the right to wrestle Nash

5) January 25, 2000 Las Vegas, Nevada Thunder aired 1/26/2000
Commissioner Kevin Nash strips Sid of the championship because he pinned the wrong Harris Brother in his championship qualifying match

6) January 25, 2000 Las Vegas, Nevada Thunder aired 1/26/2000
Commissioner Kevin Nash awards himself the championship

7) January 25, 2000 Las Vegas, Nevada Thunder aired 1/26/2000
Sid Vicious defeats Kevin Nash & Ron Harris in a triple threat steel cage match submitting Nash

8) April 10, 2000 Denver, Colorado Nitro
Vince Russo & Eric Bischoff stripped all champions of their titles rebooting WCW

9) April 16, 2000 Chicago, Illinois Spring Stampede
Jeff Jarrett defeated Diamond Dallas Page to win the vacant championship, Page had won a four man tournament (Sting, Lex Luger, & Sid) on the April 10th Nitro for the right to face Jarrett

10) April 24, 2000 Rochester, New York Nitro
Diamond Dallas Page defeated Jeff Jarrett in a steel cage match

11) April 25, 2000 Syracuse, New York Thunder aired 4/26/2000
David Arquette won the championship teaming with Diamond

Dallas Page in a tag team match against Eric Bischoff & Jeff Jarrett, the stipulation was whoever got the pin would win the title, Arquette pinned Bischoff

12) May 7, 2000 Kansas City, Missouri Slamboree
Jeff Jarrett defeated David Arquette and Diamond Dallas Page in a Triple Cage Match when Arquette turned on Page

13) May 15, 2000 Biloxi, Mississippi Nitro
"Nature Boy" Ric Flair defeated Jeff Jarrett to become the 15 time World Champion

14) May 22, 2000 Grand Rapids, Michigan Nitro
Vince Russo stripped Flair of the title, at Thunder on 5/16/2000 (aired 5/17/2000) Flair had defended his title in a handicapped match defeating Jeff Jarrett, David Flair, Crowbar, & Daffney. After the match Flair fell down leaving the ring with apparent equilibrium issues. It was later discovered to be an inner ear issue, however prior to that discovery WCW chose to vacate the title.

15) May 22, 2000 Grand Rapids, Michigan Nitro
Jeff Jarrett defeated Kevin Nash in a no holds barred match to win the vacant championship. Vince Russo tried to award Jarrett the title, however Nash stole the title leading to the match.

16) May 23, 2000 Saginaw, Michigan Thunder aired 5/24/2000
Kevin Nash defeated Jeff Jarrett & Scott Steiner in a triple threat match

17) May 29, 2000 Salt Lake City, Utah Nitro
"Nature Boy" Ric Flair is awarded the Championship by Kevin Nash who states that Flair never lost the title and it belongs to him. This is Flair's 16th and final World Championship reign

18) May 29, 2000 Salt Lake City, Utah Nitro
Jeff Jarrett defeated Ric Flair with special guest referee David Flair

19) July 9, 2000 Daytona Beach, Florida Bash at the Beach
Booker T defeated Jeff Jarrett. Earlier in the evening Jarrett was
scheduled to face Hulk Hogan for the Championship, Vince Russo
ordered Jarrett to lay down and allow Hogan to pin him, which
Jarrett did and Hogan eventually put a boot on Jarrett's chest.
After Hogan left with the belt Russo cut a scathing shoot promo on
Hogan and declared that Jarrett was still the Champion and would
defend against Booker T. Booker had lost to Kanyon earlier in the
evening when Jarrett hit Booker with a guitar. This was Hogan's
last appearance in WCW.

20) August 28, 2000 Las Cruces, New Mexico Nitro
Kevin Nash defeated Booker T

21) September 17, 2000 Buffalo, New York Fall Brawl
Booker T defeated Kevin Nash in a Caged Heat Match

22) September 25, 2000 Uniondale New York Nitro
Vince Russo defeated Booker T in a steel cage match to win the
title, yes this actually happened!

23) October 2, 2000 Daly City, California Nitro
Vince Russo decided he was not a wrestler and vacated the title

24) October 2, 2000 Daly City, California Nitro
Booker T defeated Jeff Jarrett in a San Francisco 49ers Match to
win the vacant title

25) November 26, 2000 Milwaukee, Wisconsin Mayhem
Scott Steiner defeated Booker T in a Straitjacket Steel Cage Match
to win the title

So there you have it, 25 title changes in technically just
under 11 months, two non-wrestlers held the championship, Sid
Vicious had the longest single reign at 76 days, Chris Benoit, Sid

Vicious, Diamond Dallas Page, Jeff Jarrett each held the title for 1 day whereas Kevin Nash and Ric Flair each had a reign that lasted only a couple hours. Jeff Jarrett won the championship four times but Vacated was a six time champion.

Also in the year 2000, The WCW Tag Team Championships changed hands 21 times, Hardcore Championship 19 times, Cruiserweight Championship 14 times, and United States Championship 11 times. Again, is it any wonder that this promotion folded with ridiculousness like this.

Ronnie Garvin: His NWA World Championship Matches

First published on March 7, 2019

My first memory of "Rugged" Ronnie Garvin as a kid was
when I was nine during his run in the WWE from 1988 - 1990.
Which is why I always call him "Rugged" Ronnie Garvin and not
"Hands of Stone." When I found out that he had beaten Ric Flair
for the NWA World's Championship I couldn't believe it. To me
he was a comedy wrestler, not someone that I took seriously
enough to have been World Champion. Garvin was the NWA
World Heavyweight Champion from September 25, 1987 -
November 26, 1987.

Later in life I learned to respect his in-ring ability and that
his wrestling style in WWE was nothing like his style in Mid-
Atlantic Championship Wrestling and the rest of the NWA. Sort
of how the Bushwackers were a comedy act but the Sheepherder's
were a blood and guts team.

I was always under the impression that after Garvin won
the title from Flair his first match and first defense was two months
later at Starrcade. This furthered to lower my opinion of him and
his title run. Recently I decided to look into it and see if that was
the case, and I learned that it wasn't.

Turns out he wrestled his first title match just two days

later in Greensboro against Big Bubba Rogers. He would go on to
wrestle a full load of house shows through October and November
defending the championship along the way against Ric Flair, Tully
Blanchard, Arn Anderson and others.

He also wrestled in several tag team matches teaming with
Nikita Koloff & Dusty Rhodes. He wrestled several matches on
the weekly television shows against jobbers. He even wrestled in a
War Games match at the Nassau Coliseum.

It's been said that he was just an interim champion as
Crockett wanted to have Ric Flair in a title match at Starrcade,
which was the same day as the inaugural Survivor Series, where
the fans knew Flair would win the title back. Others turned the
opportunity down except Garvin who thought it would be his only
chance to hold the championship. I have a hard time believing this
as I can't imagine anyone would turn down the opportunity to be
the NWA World Champion for even one day.

In the end though, Ronnie Garvin was a fighting champion
and even though all of his high-profile matches were on the house
shows, he still deserves our respect for his run as the NWA World
Heavyweight Champion.

List of matches with Ronnie Garvin as NWA World Champion.

September 25, 1987 JCP House Show, Detroit, Michigan
Steel Cage: Ronnie Garvin pins NWA World Champion:"Nature
Boy" Ric Flair to win the title
Garvin pinned Flair after about 35 minutes with a sunset flip off
the top rope. Footage from this match was played on World
Championship Wrestling on September 26, 1987 and on
WorldWide on October 3, 1987 the match aired with David
Crockett on commentary.

**September 27, 1987 JCP House Show, Greensboro, North
Carolina**
NWA World Champion: Ronnie Garvin defeated Big Bubba
Rogers

September 28, 1987 JCP House Show, Greenville, South Carolina
NWA World Champion: Ronnie Garvin defeated NWA Tag Team Champion: Arn Anderson

September 29 1987 JCP Television Taping. Misenheimer, North Carolina
NWA Pro - Aired October 10, 1987
NWA World Champion: Ronnie Garvin defeated Tommy Angel

Worldwide - Aired October 10, 1987
NWA World Champion: Ronnie Garvin & NWA World Television Champion: Nikita Koloff wrestled NWA Tag Team Champion: Arn Anderson & NWA United States Champion: Lex Luger to a draw

October 5, 1987 JCP House Show, Greenville, South Carolina
NWA World Champion: Ronnie Garvin defeated NWA Tag Team Champion: Tully Blanchard

October 6, 1987 JCP Television Taping, Spartanburg, South Carolina
NWA World Champion: Ronnie Garvin defeated NWA Tag Team Champion: Tully Blanchard

Worldwide - Aired October 17, 1987
NWA World Champion: Ronnie Garvin defeated jobber with Garvin Stomp

October 7, 1987 UWF TV, Cleveland, Ohio
NWA World Champion: Ronnie Garvin defeated NWA Tag Team Champion: Tully Blanchard by disqualification. Ric Flair and Lex Luger interfered with Luger ramming Garvin's head into the ringside table, busting him open. The Road Warriors and Paul Ellering made the save

October 8, 1987 JCP House Show, Hammond, Indiana
NWA World Champion: Ronnie Garvin defeated "Nature Boy"
Ric Flair

October 10, 1987 WTBS Studios Taping, Atlanta, Georgia
NWA World Champion: Ronnie Garvin pinned Mike Force

October 10, 1987 JCP House Show, Greensboro, North Carolina
NWA World Champion: Ronnie Garvin defeated "Nature Boy"
Ric Flair

October 11, 1987 JCP House Show, Cincinnati, Ohio
NWA World Champion: Ronnie Garvin defeated "Nature Boy"
Ric Flair

October 11, 1987 JCP House Show, Columbus, Ohio
NWA World Champion: Ronnie Garvin defeated "Nature Boy"
Ric Flair

October 12, 1987 JCP House Show, Greenville, South Carolina
"Nature Boy" Ric Flair & NWA United States Champion: Lex
Luger defeated NWA World Champion: Ronnie Garvin & Robert
Gibson

October 16, 1987 UWF House Show, Kansas City, Kansas
Beat 2 Out of 3 Falls: NWA World Champion: Ronnie Garvin
defeats "Nature Boy" Ric Flair

October 17, 1987 WTBS Studios Taping, Atlanta, Georgia
NWA World Champion: Ron Garvin pinned Tommy Angel
Garvin finished Angel in short fashion and cut a promo post match
about his match with Flair at Starrcade

October 17, 1987 JCP House Show, Baltimore, Maryland
NWA World Champion: Ronnie Garvin defeated "Nature Boy"
Ric Flair

October 18, 1987 JCP House Show, Detroit, Michigan
"Nature Boy" Ric Flair & NWA United States Champion: Lex
Luger defeated NWA World Champion: Ronnie Garvin &
"American Dream" Dusty Rhodes

**October 20, 1987 JCP House Show, Fayetteville, North
Carolina**
"Nature Boy" Ric Flair & NWA United States Champion: Lex
Luger defeated NWA World Champion: Ronnie Garvin &
"American Dream" Dusty Rhodes

**October 30, 1987 JCP Television Taping, Norfolk, Virginia
NWA Pro - Aired October 31, 1987**
NWA World Champion: Ronnie Garvin pinned George South,
Garvin won the match in about two minutes

Worldwide - Aired October 31, 1987
NWA World Champion: Ronnie Garvin pinned Johnny Ace,
Garvin won in 47 seconds with a punch in the face

**November 2, 1987 JCP House Show, Greenville, South
Carolina**
NWA World Champion: Ronnie Garvin pinned The Warlord

November 3, 1987 JCP House Show, Rock Hill, South Carolina
NWA World Champion: Ronnie Garvin & NWA World Television
Champion: Nikita Koloff wrestled "Nature Boy" Ric Flair & NWA
United States Champion: Lex Luger

November 4, 1987 JCP House Show, Portsmouth, Ohio
NWA World Champion: Ronnie Garvin & NWA World Television
Champion: Nikita Koloff wrestled "Nature Boy" Ric Flair & NWA

United States Champion: Lex Luger

November 7, 1987 WTBS Studios Taping, Atlanta, Georgia
NWA World Champion: Ronnie Garvin pinned Alan Martin,
Garvin beat this guy up like he owed him money, brutal.

**November 8, 1987 JCP House Show, The Omni Atlanta,
Georgia**
NWA World Champion: Ronnie Garvin defeated Gladiator #1 &
#2 in a handicap match

November 9, 1987 JCP House Show, San Francisco, California
NWA World Champion: Ronnie Garvin & Jimmy Garvin defeated
"Nature Boy" Ric Flair & NWA United States Champion: Lex
Luger

**November 12, 1987 WTBS Studios Taping, Atlanta, Georgia
Worldwide - Aired November 14, 1987**
NWA World Champion: Ronnie Garvin pinned Larry Stephens in
under two minutes with the Garvin Stomp

November 13, 1987 JCP House Show, Hampton, Virgina
NWA World Champion: Ronnie Garvin & NWA World Television
Champion: Nikita Koloff defeated "Nature Boy" Ric Flair &
NWA United States Champion: Lex Luger when Garvin pinned
Flair

November 16, 1987 JCP House Show, Inglewood, California
"Nature Boy" Ric Flair & NWA United States Champion: Lex
Luger defeated NWA World Champion: Ronnie Garvin & UWF
Heavyweight Champion: "Dr. Death" Steve Williams in an
elimination match, Garvin was pinned by Flair and Luger &
Williams were counted out of the ring.

November 21, 1987 JCP House Show, Washington DC
NWA World Champion: Ronnie Garvin defeated NWA Tag Team

Champion: Arn Anderson

November 25, 1987 JCP House Show, Long Island, New York
War Games: NWA World Champion: Ronnie Garvin, "American Dream" Dusty Rhodes, NWA Western States Heritage Champion: Barry Windham, and The Rock n' Roll Express: Ricky Morton & Robert Gibson defeated Big Bubba, NWA World Tag Team Champions: Tully Blanchard & Arn Anderson and United States Tag Team Champions: Midnight Express: Bobby Eaton & Stan Lane when Rhodes submitted Eaton with the figure four leg lock

November 26, 1987 Starrcade 1987, Chicago, Illinois
Steel Cage Match: "Nature Boy" Ric Flair pins NWA World Champion: Ronnie Garvin to win the NWA Championship

Kerry Von Erich's
NWA Championship Defenses

First published May 19, 2019

On May 6, 1984 at the David Von Erich Memorial Parade of Champions Kerry Von Erich pinned "Nature Boy" Ric Flair infront of 32,000 people at Texas Stadium to capture the NWA World Heavyweight Championship.

David had unexpectedly died just three months prior in Japan at only 25 years old. Many believed that David would one day win the world championship and that Kerry was given then honor as tribute to David.

I was just 5 years old when Kerry won the title, but when I got older I watched this match and from what I understood after Von Erich won the championship he lost it back to flair a few days later. Similar to Ronnie Garvin I never knew that Kerry defended the title, but he did.

From what I could find during his eighteen day reign he defended the title thirteen times in three different territories against six different opponents.

WCCW: World Class Championship Wrestling
CWF: Championship Wrestling from Florida
AJPW: All Japan Pro Wrestling

May 7, 1984 WCCW Fort Worth, Texas
NWA World Champion: Kerry Von Erich defeated "Bam Bam"
Terry Gordy

May 8, 1984 WCCW Muskogee, Oklahoma
NWA World Champion: Kerry Von Erich defeated "Bam Bam"
Terry Gordy

May 11, 1984 WCCW Sportatorium
NWA World Champion: Kerry Von Erich defeated "Nature Boy"
Ric Flair
I think this match is special because the Sportatorium in Dallas
was the center of the Von Erich wrestling universe and for Kerry to
step into the ring as the NWA Champion. You can find this match
on the WWE network in the vault section on the May 26, 1984
episode of World Class Championship Wrestling.

May 12, 1984 WCCW San Antonio, Texas
NWA World Champion: Kerry Von Erich defeated "Nature Boy"
Ric Flair

May 13, 1984 CWF Ocala, Florida
NWA World Champion: Kerry Von Erich wrestled Mike Rotundo
to a draw

May 13, 1984 CWF Orlando, Florida
NWA World Champion: Kerry Von Erich defeated "Superstar"
Billy Graham

May 14, 1984 CWF West Palm Beach, Florida
NWA World Champion: Kerry Von Erich defeated Ron Bass by
disqualification

May 14, 1984 CWF Fort Myers, Florida
NWA World Champion: Kerry Von Erich defeated "Superstar"

Billy Graham

May 16, 1984 CWF Miami, Florida
NWA World Champion: Kerry Von Erich defeated "Superstar"
Billy Graham by disqualification

May 18, 1984 CWF Lake City, Florida
NWA World Champion: Kerry Von Erich defeated "Superstar"
Billy Graham

May 19, 1984 CWF Tampa, Florida
NWA World Champion: Kerry Von Erich defeated Ron Bass by
disqualification

May 22, 1984 AJPW Tokyo, Japan
NWA World Champion: Kerry Von Erich wrestled Jumbo Tsuruta
in a 2 of 3 falls match to a draw at one fall each
You can find this match on youtube and it's pretty high quality.

May 14, 1984 AJPW Kanagawa, Japan
"Nature Boy" Ric Flair defeated NWA World Champion: Kerry
Von Erich 2 falls to 1 to win the Championship

Pedro Morales: One The Greatest Champions in WWE History

First published on February 11, 2019

Pedro Morales is one of the greatest champions in the history of the WWE and I'm going to tell you why. I didn't always think so when I was a kid whenever Pedro was on TV I remember him losing or getting wins over jobbers who I called bums. I would hear the commentators state that he was a former champion, but I just didn't see it. Now looking back and seeing his old matches I see it and you should too.

Born in 1942 he debuted at the age of 17 in 1959 in New York after training with Barba Roja. Although primarily known by me for being in the now WWE he has stints all over the United States and in Japan.

He held titles in NWA Hawaii, Championship Wrestling from Florida, NWA San Francisco, Puerto Rico's WWC and was a two time WWA World Heavyweight Champion. He also wrestled for the American Wrestling Association, Crockett's Mid-Atlantic Championship Wrestling, New Japan Pro Wrestling, as well as other promotions.

On January 24, 1963 the Capitol Wrestling Corporation

officially became the WWWE holding their first ever television
taping in Bridgeport, Connecticut on January 29th. Morales made
his WWE debut at that taping, teaming with Dory Dixon and
defeated Johnny Barend & The Magnificent Maurice. He stayed
with the WWE for two years then moved onto the WWA.

On February 8, 1971 at Madison Square Garden Morales
defeated Ivan Koloff for the WWWE World Heavyweight
Championship ending the Russian Bears three week reign as
champion. He would go on to hold the championship for 1,027
days, dropping it to Stan "The Man" Stasiak in Philadelphia,
Pennsylvania on December 1, 1973.

As champion he headlined Madison Square Garden 30
times defending his title against the likes of Larry Hennig,
BlackJack Mulligan, Freddie Blassie, Ray Stevens, and George
"The Animal" Steele just to name a few. On September 30, 1972
Morales defended the Championship against Bruno Sammartino in
front of more than 22,000 fans at Shea Stadium wrestling to a 75
minute time limit draw.

Morales left the WWE in 1975 returning in 1980. On
August 9, 1980 he and then WWE Champion Bob Backlund
defeated the Wild Samoans in two straight falls to win the World
Tag Team Championships. They were stripped of the titles the
next day because of Backlund being the WWE Champion.

On December 8, 1980 he defeated Ken Patera at Madison

Square Garden to capture the Intercontinental Heavyweight Championship becoming the first ever Triple Crown Champion. He would hold the championship for 194 daus dropping it to Don Muraco in Philadelphia on June 20, 1981, but would regain it from Muraco on November 23rd at MSG.

His second reign would last over a year until January 22, 1983 when Muraco defeated him again at the Garden ending Morales' 425 day run.

To summarize:

Morales is the first ever Triple Crown Champion

He is one of only two people to ever hold the World and Intercontinental Championships for over a year in a single reign, the other is "Macho Man" Randy Savage.

His 1,027 days as World Champion is the fifth longest single reign behind Bruno's two reigns, Bob Backlund, & Hulk Hogan. As Intercontinental Champion he held the title twice for a combined 619 days, the longest reigning champion of all time. His second reign at 425 days is the second longest single reign behind the Honky Tonk Man.

Some will argue that I'm wrong, for instance Chris Jericho has held every championship in the promotion. WWE Champion, World Champion, World Heavyweight Champion, Hardcore Champion, European Champion, Intercontinental Champion, United States Champion, WWE Tag Team Champion, and World Tag Team Champion.

In total Jericho had 26 championship reigns whereas Morales only had four. However, Morales' four reigns lasted for 1,647 days and Jericho's twenty six lasted 1,059 days. I firmly believe that this proves that Pedro Morales, without question, is one of the greatest champions in the history of the WWE.

Tito Santana vs. Greg Valentine

First published April 25, 2020

For reasons unknown I just had the urge to watch a classic feud from my childhood, one that is underrated and doesn't get talked about enough, Tito Santana and Greg "The Hammer" Valentine's battle over the Intercontinental Heavyweight Championship.

Tito first won the championship from Don Muraco on February 11, 1984 in Boston, MA at the Garden. He held the title for 226 days, losing it to Valentine in London, Ontario for Maple Leaf Wrestling on September 24, 1984. Valentine would hold the title for 285 days when Santana regained it inside a Steel Cage on July 6, 1985 in Baltimore, Maryland. Santana's second and final reign came to an end on February 8, 1986 in the city he first won it, Boston, when "Macho" Man Randy Savage captured the crown.

I checked the Old School section on the WWE Network and much to my surprise none of the Santana vs. Valentine matches are on it. I check All Star Wrestling, Prime Time Wrestling, and even Tuesday Night Titans and only TNT has episodes from 1984 / 1985 and none of them featured the title change.

How could this be!?! Whenever a title change took place Gorilla Monsoon would say, history has been made, and yet the WWE doesn't have footage of these matches on their network.

The matches are on YouTube!

Digging deeper into the WWE Network if you go to the section In Ring, then WWE Home Video Classics, look for Match Compilations and finally WWE Grudge Match Mar 27, 1986. This is an old coliseum home video release. This tape has three segments looking at the feud between Valentine & Santana starting with Valentine winning the championship from Tito and ending with their cage match from Baltimore where Santana recaptured the title.

September 24, 1984 London, Ontario, Canada
Intercontinental Champion: Tito Santana vs. Greg "The Hammer" Valentine
On Grudge Matches this match is clipped down to four minutes, YouTube has the complete match.

July 6, 1985 in Baltimore, Maryland
Steel Cage Match: Intercontinental Champion: Greg "The Hammer" Valentine vs Tito Santana
This match is very significant as after Santana won the championship Valentine destroyed the championship belt on the cage. WWE would then introduce the version of the Championship that most people are familiar with.
In an interview from a couple years ago Santana was asked what happened to the broken championship and he replied that he threw it in the trash that night at the arena in Baltimore.
On the WWE Network if you search Tito Santana vs. Greg Valentine there are 12 matches that come back featuring both men, some are tag matches but there are four in particular that I want to point out.

TNT: Tuesday Night Titans July 17, 1984
Santana is Champion and this features a non-title match between the two. Valentine is interviewed by McMahon before and after the match and it's worth watching

WWE Old School October 22, 1984, at Madison Square Garden

Valentine is champion, this match is short but they beat the hell out of each other! Also it sets up the return match that happened the next month. This is also Santana's first match back after surgery on his knee, also his return match against Valentine after losing the championship to him in September. Valentine injured Tito causing him to have the surgery.

WWE Old School November 26, 1984 at Madison Square Garden

Valentine is champion and this is the best match between the two on the card during this time frame. It goes nearly thirty minutes and really shows that these guys can work their ass off. This match was the main event of the card, Hogan was not on the show, and it was a sell out. That's how big this feud was they main evented and sold out Madison Square Garden.

WWE Old School March 17, 1985 at Madison Square Garden

Valentine is champion and this is a Lumberjack match but it's really not the over the top Lumberjack style match that I am used to that WWE has put out the last 20 years.

My overall reaction to these series of matches is that these guys beat the hell out of each other every time they were in the ring together. A lot of people only know Tito for his time in the WWE in the 1990's and they are missing out on what he could do in the ring.

Santana and Valentine were first in the ring together Mid-Atlantic Championship Wrestling on December 3, 1978 in Charlotte, North Carolina. Granted this was a 24 man battle royal, but I'd like to think that they mixed it up. Six months later they were in another battle royal together, this time for the WWE at Madison Square Garden on June 4, 1979.

They wouldn't be in the ring together again until March 31, 1984 at the Spectrum in Philadelphia. In this match Santana was defending his Intercontinental Championship against Valentine and the match ended in a time limit draw. The most recent match against each other was an amazing 33 years later, on February 25, 2017 for the Superstars of Wrestling Federation in Totowa, New Jersey where they battled to a no contest!

Currently Santana is 66 years old and Valentine is 68 years old and they both had matches in late 2019. If they wrestled against each other again this year I'd watch it.

The Fabulous Freebirds Unique WCW Tag Team Championship Reign

First published on June 15, 2016

Recently while researching my blog post One Day Champions I came across a very odd match listing and I just had to share it here. On February 18, 1991 in Montgomery, Alabama The Fabulous Freebirds: Michael PS Hayes and Jimmy "Jam" Garvin lost the WCW World Tag Team Championships to Rick and Scott The Steiner Brothers. I know what you are thinking, one team losing tag titles to another team isn't that unusual, in fact it has happened hundreds of times. What makes this unique is the next entry in the title lineage.

February 24, 1991 Wrestle War 91 Phoenix, AZ Veterans Memorial Coliseum Michael Hayes & Jimmy Garvin with Big Daddy Dink defeated WCW Tag Team Champions Doom with Teddy Long to win the titles at 6:57 when Garvin pinned Simmons after Reed accidentally hit his partner with a foreign object thrown in the ring by Long, with Dink then shoving Garvin onto Simmons for the win; prior to the bout, the challengers were escorted to the ring by Diamond Dallas Page who then introduced Dink as the Freebirds' "road boss" before leaving ringside; after the match, DDP and the Diamond Dolls returned ringside and celebrated with the new champions as Reed assaulted Simmons with the weapon and left the ring with Long.

Yes you read that correctly they lost the titles 6 days before they won them making the Fabulous Freebirds that only Champions whose title run was negative days. It was literally over before it began! I realize that the match that was held on February 18th was taped for television and didn't air until March 9th, however they still technically lost the titles before even winning them.

This incident is a result of WCW and their odd television taping schedule for their syndicated shows which they taped several weeks in advance. I recall reading in Mick Foley's book about how he watched the team of Pretty Wonderful: Paul Roma & Paul Orndorff cutting a promo about beating Cactus Jack & Kevin Sullivan for the tag team championships before Cactus and Sullivan had even won them.

What's even more interesting to me is that according to The History of WWE Doom would defend the titles at house shows between the 18th & 24th while The Freebirds were billed as tag team champions at house shows between the February 24th and March 9th. At the end of the day though, officially the Fabulous Freebirds were Tag Team Champions for negative six days.

www.ingramcontent.com/pod-product-compliance
Lightning Source LLC
Chambersburg PA
CBHW031128130726
47988CB00006B/2271

9 798665 111988